I0126903

SEEING

BEYOND DREAMING TO RELIGIOUS EXPERIENCES OF LIGHT

George Gillespie

ia

imprint-academic.com

Copyright © George Gillespie, 2019

The moral rights of the author have been asserted.
No part of this publication may be reproduced in any form
without permission, except for the quotation of brief passages
in criticism and discussion.

Published in the UK by
Imprint Academic Ltd., PO Box 200, Exeter EX5 5YX, UK

Distributed in the USA by
Ingram Book Company,
One Ingram Blvd., La Vergne, TN 37086, USA

ISBN 9781788360098 paperback

A CIP catalogue record for this book is available from the
British Library and US Library of Congress

To Charlotte, who encouraged me,
spoiled me, and made it possible
for me to do this work.

Contents

Preface

I grew up trying to follow Jesus and to love God and neighbor. I knew next to nothing about mysticism, and as far as I remember, even in seminary, Berkeley Baptist Divinity School (now the American Baptist Seminary of the West), knowing the mystics was not a part of the curriculum. Technically, somehow I became what they call a "mystic," I think it is fair to say, but I'm actually hesitant to say that. I remember reading that Robert Frost was always hesitant to call himself a poet. He felt that "poet" was a complimentary word to call someone, and it was up to someone else to call you that. That is how I really feel about the word "mystic."

In preparation for the unexpected experiences that I think of as mystical, I had no teacher, guru, or spiritual director. I was in no monastic tradition. I was (and am still) a Baptist. I had no theories about mystical experience, and knew closely only the examples from the Bible—the stories of Saul on the road to Damascus, of John being in the spirit on the Lord's day, Jacob and his dream of the ladder to heaven, the visions of the prophets, and the transfiguration of Jesus seen by a few disciples. When things began to happen to me, I was on my own.

After rewriting this story again and again—after trying to be clearer and clearer in expressing myself—more clear than it seems possible to be—this small book is the testimony that I end up with. I thank God that I have reached an old age and have been able to endlessly rewrite. But I must stop sometime.

Chapters I and II present the bare bones of the narrative, if I can call it that. Chapter I tells the beginnings of my lucid dreaming (knowing that I am dreaming while still dreaming) and then the religious experiences of God in the fullness of light. Chapter II describes a point in which a "near-death" experience becomes my last encounter with the fullness of light.

Chapter III tells about many later experiences of hypnopompic lattice imagery, in which I was able to study the imagery and learn how the lattice image, and thus visual imagery in general, is constructed internally, seen, and scanned. I've discovered also how, with my perceptual mindset, I see the image three-dimensionally. Chapter III was not easy to write and it is, I have heard, not easy to understand the concepts that I hope to describe. Please do not get stuck trying to get through Chapter III. If need be, skip it and go on to Chapter IV. You can go back to Chapter III later. I wish to keep Chapter III there because it helps to explain the experiences of the fullness of light, which I go on to analyze after that.

Chapters IV, V, and VI then finish the study of the fullness of light. Chapter IV covers dreaming, for the light experience grows out of the context of dreams, even though the light itself is not a dream image. Dreamed body imagery may continue for some time into the experience of God in the light. In Chapter V, we study light itself, which has a special place in this story, and in Chapter VI we study what I mean when I talk about the presence of God.

I don't know why I have been blessed with lucid dreams, the experiences of the fullness of light, and then later lattice hypnopompic imagery, along with a lot of other forms of visual imagery that do not fit into this story. However, I feel responsible for telling what I have learned from all this, and I hope that I have been able to make somewhat clear all the difficult parts.

My thanks to Fred Smith, David Scott, Scott Sparrow, and Charlotte Gillespie for reading earlier versions of this manuscript and making helpful comments. I want to especially thank Dr. Harry T. Hunt, who often offered advice, encouragement, and serious challenges throughout the writing of this work and many previous writings. I feel that I have been able to make major improvements in concepts and wording during these years due to his responses to what I showed him. We did not get to see each other much, but what he said to me was important. Thank you, Harry.

Sleep

---

1. Amazing Grace

I dreamed I was back in India looking for something. I came to the door of a room. This was the place I was looking for. As I went in, I faced a wall, which I knew to be part of a large cube reaching from floor to ceiling. The cube was part of the construction of the building. I had to walk around it to get to the inner room. The passageway around was fairly dark. The situation seemed odd and I realized I was dreaming. I walked around the left side of the cube, past corrugated iron roofing sheets (as commonly used in India), which were stored there, and piles of sawdust, and came to the inner room.

I found in the inner room a group of poor Christian laborers from the tea plantations. They were people that I was familiar with from years of work in Assam, in the northeast corner of India, where many Christians in the Brahmaputra Valley pick tea leaves for a living. We were glad to see each other. I still knew I was dreaming and felt, therefore, that I should do something. I suggested that we sing "Amazing Grace." We all then slowly and heartily sang the hymn in English, while I directed the singing with my hand. I knew it didn't matter how well I directed, since this was a dream.

We began to sing, "Amazing grace—how sweet the sound—that saved a wretch like me." I had no trouble remembering the words of the first verse, which is all we sang. I watched to see how well the movement of the mouths of the people was coordinated with the sounds of the words (this being a dream). Their mouths moved somewhat with the music, but not precisely. I saw that Charlotte, my wife, was also singing next to me. We sang on loudly and grandly, "I once was lost, but now am found, was blind, but now I see." The experience was intensely devotional.

When the verse was over, I tried to think of what to do next. I considered leading the group in the Lord's Prayer, but thought it might take too long, and I would probably wake up before we finished. As I thought about what to do, I saw that a light was shining high in front of me like a brilliant sun. I recognized this kind of light from previous experiences. Then, while the sun itself remained in view, intense light spread throughout the entire visual field. All other visual imagery disappeared. I was aware that God was present and began shouting, "God is love." My devotion was spontaneous, joyful, and profound. Barely had I called out "God is love" a couple of times, I decided to think the phrase calmly to myself instead. While I then silently repeated within myself "God is love" over and over, I felt myself gradually rise up into the air. The light surrounding me remained intense, and I worshiped in this way for some time before I woke up.

The experience of knowing I am dreaming is commonly called "lucid dreaming." I had been having lucid dreams off and on frequently for about seven years at the time of this experience. However, experiences of the presence of God in light were a more recent development and uncommon for me. This one came to me July 18, 1982, while I was living in Moorestown, New Jersey. This was my fourth experience of what I came to call "the fullness of light." When I woke up and reflected on what had happened, I thought of the experience, as I usually did at that time, not as a truly mystical experience, although I knew it was like one, but as the concluding part of the dream.

Many unusual things have happened in my lucid dreams, and I was used to looking at my dreams analytically after I woke up. Perhaps if I had had no previous experience with lucid dreams and had simply settled into prayer while awake, and, in the midst of prayer, the light had suddenly over-whelmed me and I came to feel the presence of God, I would have accepted immediately that the experience was self-evident—that it was the kind of spiritual event that people call "mystical." But the light did not come while I was awake or during prayer. During the experience, I believed that I was in the presence of God. After I woke up, I believed, as usual, that I had dreamed it, because I had been asleep.

In time I came to struggle between my waking rational view that such experiences of mine were simply dreamed and my less rational wish to acknowledge my unquestioning acceptance of the experiences while they were happening as authentically knowing the presence of God. In time, I began to see evidence that the image of light during the fullness is different from dream imagery in important ways—that is, that my experiences of God in light happened beyond dreaming. As the reader will see, light has become an important part of my sleep experience and has occupied a primary place in my mind and in my writing (see Gillespie, 1992, 2009, 2014). These experiences of light and the circumstances surrounding them were the inspiration for my beginning to write this testimony.

Even now, more than thirty years after the experience that I told here, I do not trust myself to sing "Amazing Grace" in church all the way through, for the memory of that moment of grace rises in my throat and chokes off my voice.

2. My Spiritual Work

This account of religious experiences of light and of much more records a search for truth. I am by nature an analytical person, so that when I analyze in detail such matters as dreams, visual imagery, and awareness of the presence of God in light, I am reacting naturally to what happens to me. Over time, analyzing has become my spiritual work. I have no intention of explaining away the experiences of God in light or other matters of the spirit. Like a scientist, I want to find out what is true, but I consider the search for truth through dreams, hypnopompic geometric imagery, and light to be a spiritual search. I know that the concepts I write about are difficult, and I wish my readers well.

The scientist works in the world of common experience, with bodies, brains, plants, neurons, molecules, and "facts," where one's work is open to criticism and confirmation by others. Subjective experiences, such as I examine in this testimony, are too private, individualistic, and unconfirmable for a normal scientific approach. Scientists appear to prefer studying such private experiences only indirectly, such as by studying the brain or by gathering statistics. I have been able to study them firsthand.

There are invisibles, such as God and spirit, which lie not only outside of public view, but beyond my own direct experience. I find that my own experience of God, which seems to be direct, upon my analysis is actually indirect. But there are other things, such as dreams and experiences of light, which, although they lie outside of public view, do lie within my view, and I can study them. For example, although God exists beyond my seeing and touching, my "experience of the presence of God" lies within my experience. I can study what I see, what I feel, and how I understand it at the time. I can study how the visual image is constructed and experienced. I can study light as visual image. I can also connect my analysis to what else is said by others about how the world works.

The subjective experiences that I describe in this writing are not directly available for scientific study, because they exist only for me. But neither are they simply matters of faith, for I actually do see dream imagery, color, visual form, darkness, and light. I do feel numinosity, reverence, and joy. These are some of the facts of subjective experience. The private experiences that I describe lie between what the scientist investigates and what is totally a matter of faith. They lie in what I think of as a middle category between science and faith, between what is public and what is invisible and inaccessible even to me at all times.

When I began to have lucid dreams and then religious experiences of light, I had little idea about introspection and phenomenology and did not know their history. However, from the beginning, I had in mind certain principles as I wrote about and analyzed these private phenomena. I was on my own and the following approaches, although I did not spell them out at the time or even think them through, generally seemed right to me:

1. To make all final analysis of dream and related events when fully awake. When I know I am dreaming, I can experiment and observe, but I find that I do not necessarily have insight while I am dreaming.
2. To assume that my understanding of what I see during the experience is part of the data and does not necessarily explain what I see.
3. To recognize that inner visual experiences, such as seeing dreams or light, may have no necessary parallels to how my body sees while I am awake. During waking analysis, I did not automatically apply the perceptual paradigm of retinas, light waves, reflecting surfaces, and three-dimensionality to inner experience.

4. To not be misled by the awesome, even in religious experience. Awe during an experience is beyond my control. But
   after the experience, I wanted to be careful in my analysis.
5. To be precise in detail as far as I can when I write down
   what happened.
6. To be modest in my vocabulary.

I hope that I have lived largely up to these principles through
the years. Until starting to put together this manuscript, my
published writing had mostly focused on my analytical work
with dreams, hypnopompic imagery, perception, and varieties
of these subjects and not so much on my religious experience,
which I was reluctant at first to talk much about. I did, in fact,
end up writing one article that was for me a short religious
testimony (Gillespie, 1988). It is only in more recent years that I
have felt able, in fact compelled, to finally write about these
matters in detail as a believer, combining religious faith with (I
hope) careful observation. I analyze and criticize my religious
experiences, such as those I tell about here, not because I don't
believe in authentic religious experience, but because I do
believe.

A lot of what I write about is concerned with light. In fact,
my original title for this manuscript was "A Testimony to
Light." Although I want to be careful with how I say things, I
cannot avoid using the word "light" to mean two different
things, as is common in the way people talk. There is the light
that comes from the sun and passes through space, at "the
speed of light," that exists as both waves and particles. This is
the external light that reaches the eye and stops at the retina.

The other is the light that I see. It is the subjective experience
of brightness. I think "I see light" when something in the
environment or in a dream is bright enough to call light.
Subjective light, that is, the experience of brightness, is internal.
It is visual image and does not move through space. It has no

speed or wavelength. This distinction is worth mentioning here, in order to lessen the confusion, I hope, in reading this.

Although this story starts out as a religious narrative, it ends up as much more. It is more, because so much of religious experience does not have religious explanations. How visual imagery, dreaming, and visual perception work must also be taken into account to understand my religious experiences of light, and I have been able to investigate these things. In the end I find that thinking, learning, and correcting what I have written are endless. Therefore, what I have done here will be finished only by stopping.

3. The Beginning

It is through lucid dreaming that I came to know the presence of God in the fullness of light. My lucid dreaming began with this dream:

> As I came out of the jungle, I came to a missionary bungalow. It seemed to me that I was in either India or Africa. I told the couple who came to the door that I was only dreaming and wanted to know where I was before I woke up. They said nothing. I went into the house and looked for maps that might indicate where I was. I found maps with names that could have been Indian, but I could not be certain. In another room, I found two friends from my student days at seminary in Berkeley. I told them about my search. They did not respond. I thought at the time, You know, I can just open my eyes and make you disappear. However, I did not open my eyes. Then I woke up.

I had never heard of dreams in which the dreamer was aware of dreaming. I was impressed. That first lucid dream came to me spontaneously in 1975 while Charlotte and I were living in India. We were American Baptist missionaries teaching at Eastern Theological College in the town of Jorhat in the state of

Assam, about 50 miles from the Burma border. I could not know then that this dream was the beginning of unique experiences that would teach me so much, repeatedly challenge my thinking, and eventually lead to the events that I describe and analyze in these pages. I did not suspect that I was at the beginning of a spiritual journey. I was 42. And with this dream began the second half of my life.

How do I account for my spontaneous leap into lucid dreaming at that time? I do not know, but this, I suspect, is part of the reason. When I was 40, I thought that it was about time for me to begin some routine of physical exercise. India had been my home since 1959. So I had often heard and read of the physical benefits of yoga and knew well its spiritual context. I knew that yoga, though primarily a Hindu practice, is not, as a physical and mental process, necessarily limited to any one philosophical system or any one religious goal. Some Christians practice yoga, both as a physical and a spiritual practice, with Christian goals. So I decided to do the physical exercises that are a part of yoga.

As a start, I bought in the bazar some small Indian books on yoga. Later, during a stay in the United States, I also found J.-M. Déchanet's book, *Christian Yoga* (1960), and this remained my guide for some years. Déchanet's book started me on using Christian scripture verses as part of my yoga practice.

As I progressed with the exercises, I gradually was able to keep my body in different difficult positions, working slowly, calmly, and without strain. I found that calm concentration on the physical postures was also calm concentration of the mind. I believe that practicing yoga over time helped to prepare me in some small way, perhaps, to work on my inner life and gave me a calmness and balance of mind that helped to make me ready for lucid dreaming. I do not believe that yoga could have been the major factor. In any case, since lucid dreaming began spontaneously, I must have been ready for it.

When lucid dreaming began, I saw it as an opportunity to study the nature of dreaming. After five lucid dreams, I began to plan experiments to carry out when I knew I was dreaming. I planned while awake, so that for every lucid dream I had an experiment ready to carry through if I could recall in the dream what it was I had planned to do.

I tested the solidity of dream objects by first feeling them as I feel objects when I am awake and then by putting my hand through them. I could do both, as I wished. When I put my hand through objects, I could feel the objects as my hand easily passed through them. I planned ahead a dream story to see whether I could carry it through. The story that I planned was for me to find a greenhouse and go in and buy a plant. I eventually was able to do that with some unexpected elements. For example, the salesman that I anticipated turned out to be a woman. To test my mental ability, I tried to put into alphabetical order what I saw in the dream. This was always fairly easy. I often tried to remember where I was sleeping. I never could remember. For the first five or six years of frequent lucid dreams, this was the direction of my thinking, and the kinds of things I tested. About half the time, when I discovered I was dreaming, I could remember what I had intended to do and did it.

After 17 lucid dreams, I saw in the fourteenth edition of the *Encyclopaedia Britannica*, which I found in the college library, an article on dreams with a simple statement about two men who told of knowing they were dreaming. There were no further details. This was the first I knew that others had reported such dreams.

As I saw no discussion of lucid dreams anywhere, I developed my own understanding of them, and when I wrote them down, which I did regularly, I first called them "known dreams." In 1977, soon after moving from Jorhat to teach at Andhra Christian Theological College in the city of Hyderabad in South India, I found Ann Faraday's *Dream Power* (1972) in a book store in that city. After 48 "known dreams," I had found a discussion of lucid dreams for the first time.

It was not until we arrived in the United States in the summer of 1979 and settled in Moorestown, New Jersey, that I came in touch with more literature on lucid dreaming, which was then still very scarce and mostly Western. I then adopted the commonly-used term "lucid dream" in my own writing about my dreams. My lack of familiarity with what was being said and done in the field of lucid dreaming during those first few years laid a basis, I feel, for an independent approach to understanding the nature, value, and meaning of such dreams. Light played no part in my dream experiences during those early years.

4. Stained Glass

I occasionally experience colors in lucid dreams that are much more intense than they ever are in ordinary dreams or even in daytime perception. Some other lucid dreamers have reported this also (Kelzer, 1987; LaBerge & Rheingold, 1990). I notice this intensity during the dream itself, and sometimes my noticing is what leads me to realize that I am dreaming.

> (May 7, 1988) I was returning to live in northeast India. While walking in the Garo Hills with some Garo and other tribal people, I came to a bridge across a small river. The hills and jungle along the river were strikingly bright, as also the river and everything else. Having in mind that I had just met Rev. Singha who was supposed to have died and that the scene was unrealistically bright, I realized I was dreaming. I continued to talk to the people on the bridge, and there was no further change in color. All that I saw had the brightness of a stained-glass window with cloudless sunlight coming from behind it. The world looked trans-lucent, and not as if everything simply reflected sunlight. Everything was the right color, only more intense.

Aldous Huxley (1990) reported that when he took the drug mescaline he saw flowers in his room shining, as he said, as if from their own inner light. The books in his room glowed with bright colors and great meaning. Huxley was awake and took the intense glowing to be a quality of the things themselves, with the mescaline making it possible for him to see their inner significance. What Huxley describes is precisely what has been my experience with the intense brightening of some lucid dreams.

I believe that what was produced in Huxley's visual field upon taking mescaline and within my own visual field during lucid dreaming is the same process—the intensification of the image-making properties of the visual field, in his case during visual perception, and in my case during lucid dreaming.

5. Window Light

Long before I began to have lucid dreams, I occasionally woke up and felt paralyzed. This has happened at the end of an afternoon nap and sometimes in the night. It never concerned me, because I was used to it. This has happened off and on until the present, although less frequently now. When I wake up paralyzed, although I am awake, my body feels "asleep" and I cannot move it. I tend not to open my eyes. I am usually lying on my back. Then I feel myself slowly separating from my body that is lying on the bed, one part of me at a time.

First my feet rise up, then the arms, then the rest of the body, until I feel myself float up and away, on my back, it seems, face up. Then I am projected involuntarily at great speed head first, hearing and feeling a great buzz that seems to be located inside my head and feeling the wind brush against my body and clothes. I most often remain face-up, but sometimes am face-down. The "trip" may finish with the sensation of falling back into my body on the bed.

The experience feels totally real. During the flight, I have always accepted that I might really be going somewhere, and I would think of visiting somewhere specific, such as my sister Jeanne's house. But I never saw any signs that I had really done so. Nowadays, this experience is commonly called an out-of-body experience, and there are people who try to do it. I never made it happen, but I would let it happen. In the context of mysticism, I believe the experience is referred to as a "flight of the spirit" and/or is associated with rapture. Teresa of Avila (1979) refers to her own "flights of the spirit" in the context of her mystical experiences. However, these were never religious experiences for me.

I believe that the realistic feeling of rising out of the body explains the Apostle Paul's comment about what was probably his own experience when he says,

> I know a person in Christ who fourteen years ago was caught up to the third heaven — whether in the body or out of the body I do not know; God knows. And I know that such a person — whether in the body or out of the body I do not know; God knows — was caught up into Paradise and heard things that are not to be told, that no mortal is permitted to repeat. (II Corinthians 12:2-4; all quotations from the Bible are from the New Revised Standard Version)

First, I am the body lying on the bed. Although the body feels paralyzed, I am aware of it. As I separate from the body on the bed, I am aware of being the part of my body that has separated, but I also know that my body is still lying in bed. Finally, I am aware of being totally separated bodily. I no longer feel the body lying on the bed, but I understand that it is still there. I also know that I am now floating up.

After I began having lucid dreams, the out-of-body sensation occasionally became a part of a lucid dream. If, during a lucid dream, I shut my eyes and concentrate my attention away from my body imagery, my attachment to the ground may disappear. Occasionally I then feel my legs rise up in front of me, and I lose contact with the (dreamed) ground or floor. Then I become aware of floating. Sometimes I then speed off in the usual out-of-body sensation. The projected body is in continuity with the body imagery that I had been dreaming.

There is a difference between beginning the experience upon waking up in bed and beginning it while dreaming. When I wake up and feel my body paralyzed, I feel what appears to be the separation of my dreamed body from my body in bed. When this happens in a dream, I do not feel my body separate from my dreamed or my sleeping body. I take this to be because, upon falling asleep and dreaming, I have already left behind the awareness of my everyday body. So in a dream, I may just float up and buzz away.

In a dream (March 9, 1979), I found a simple Indian country boat to travel in, a common kind of boat in India. The boat was long and low, not rising much above the water. A man began rowing me across the water, which spread in every direction, as during a flood. For some reason I realized that I was dreaming. I thought that, since I was dreaming, I could travel across the water without the boat. I then moved across the water boatless and soon I was projected off at great speed across the water, face-down and feeling the elements brushing past me and hearing and feeling the great buzz in my head. This was the usual out-of-body feeling, but I thought of it as going across the water instead of through the air, although I did not feel the water. It felt like air. I was passive. I didn't fly actively, and I was not moving my legs or arms.

I remembered reading in the out-of-body literature that if you opened your eyes during an out-of-body experience, you may see that you are in some other actual waking place. I was still flying head forward with my body facing down. I opened my (dreamed) eyes (which I would think were already open). I was still flying, but I could not discern much ahead of me. However, when I turned my eyes (not my head) to look below myself and toward the back, I noticed a pair of windows lit up behind me, beyond my feet, to the left. The rest of the visual field was dark. The pair of windows next to each other maintained their look, size, and spatial relationship to me beyond my feet, even though it seemed I was flying away from the windows at great speed. That was all I could see, other than darkness.

After some time, I woke up on my back, and the two windows of my room, which were lit up, compared to the darkness of the room, were there where I could see them directly if I turned my eyes (and not my head) down and looked a bit to the left beyond the position of my feet. When I saw the windows after I had awakened into my bedroom, my eyes were turned exactly in the same position as they had been turned while I was dreaming. I had seen my bedroom windows in the out-of-body dream. Curtains and other objects between me and the windows influenced the shape of the outline of my windows in the same way in the dream and while awake.

Whether I had seen the light of my bedroom windows through my eyelids or not, I do not know. I had been seeing the windows from the viewpoint of the eyes of my body lying on my back in bed while I dreamed that I was seeing the windows while I was traveling through the air face down. I had not been seeing from the eyes of a flying dream body. This was a case (and not the first one) in which some element of my visual field for dreaming proved to be also my visual field for perception. I will not judge other people's claim that they had actually traveled off through space while projecting "out-of-body" and seen other places, but for me I realized that, because of my continued view of the window before and after dreaming, this time at least I had gone nowhere while feeling that I was projected forward at great speed.

Nelson Pike (1992), in his analytical study of the experiences of rapture of Teresa of Avila, finds that Teresa uses the word "soul" in two manners. First is the soul as a dwelling place within her where certain mystical experiences happen. The other use is the soul as herself when she is having her experiences. For example, Teresa repeatedly says that it is her soul, in its second meaning of the word, that gets lifted up seemingly out of her body during rapture until it is engulfed by God. The out-of-body experience is of the soul. Since it is commonly said that the soul leaves the body when one dies, Pike notes that "[t]o claim that the soul really does leave the body would appear to conflict with the obvious fact that the mystic does not suffer physical death in the process" (1992, p. 15). In the end, Teresa herself actually does not know what to say about whether or not the soul leaves the body in rapture.

It never occurred to me to use the word "soul" in any description of my experiences. I wouldn't unless I had a precise idea of how to use the word, and I don't. In any case, I have identified the out-of-body body with the body that I dream. It would not have occurred to me to say that it is my soul who appears in dreams.

Patricia Garfield reports her version of what I speak of as "hearing and feeling the great buzz in the head." She reports that in a dream, "I begin to feel slightly dizzy (the lightheadedness) and I rise up into the air. Now my body is a-tremble with a 'sound-feel.' It is a tactile-noise, or an audible-touch—both at once" (1979, p. 152). This sound-feel is a familiar sensation in her lucid dreams, while I associate that sensation only with the "out-of-body" experience of seeming to project through space.

6. Dreamless Sleep

I taught courses on Indian religions at the college in Jorhat and again in Hyderabad, and, along with my own reading, I grew in my understanding of Hindu religious and philosophical concepts. I was familiar with the Hindu discussions of the four states of consciousness, as found in the Upanishads and their commentaries.

In the earliest Upanishads, dated variously from 800 BCE to 200 CE, it is said that the state of consciousness farthest from what is ultimately real is the waking state. Next comes the dream state, which is also illusion. In dreams, the dreamer dreams by his own light. Beyond dreams, there lies the third state, the state of dreamless sleep, sometimes called just "sleep" or "deep sleep." The person asleep "desires no desire and sees no dream" (*Bṛhadāraṇyaka Upaniṣad* 4.3.19; unless otherwise noted, all translations from the Sanskrit are my own).

Those who follow Advaita Vedanta consider dreamless sleep to consist of pure objectless consciousness. S.K. Saksena explains:

> That the seeming appearance of unconsciousness in deep sleep is due to the absence of objects and not to the absence of consciousness, is almost generally acknowledged. There is, therefore, no inconsistency in accepting consciousness as the essence of self, and yet postulating a self in deep sleep which is unconscious of anything… (1971, pp. 124–125)

In any case, dreamless sleep is the doorway to the fourth state, called *turīya*, which is "unseen, unrelated, incomprehensible, without distinctive marks, unthinkable, indescribable, whose essence is the knowledge of the one Self, the cessation of manifestation, peaceful, auspicious, and nondual" (*Māṇḍūkya Upaniṣad* 7). To achieve the fourth state is liberation from endless rebirths. I saw that dreamless sleep cannot be just a Hindu state of consciousness, but a supposed state common to all humankind about which Hindus believe something. The ancient Indian seers found dreamless sleep to be an important subject of discussion.

During my twenty years of life in India, my own theology was nurtured in the Indian Christian context, and I was interested in the Hindu understanding of the four states of consciousness. I was drawn to the writings of Indian Christian theologians who discuss Christianity in Indian terms (see Boyd, 1975) and the writing of such people as Sadhu Sundar Singh, the Christian sadhu (see Heiler, 1970), and Swami Abhishiktananda, the French Benedictine monk, who found spiritual insight in the Upanishads (Abhishiktananda, 1974, 1975, 1976, and other writings).

After returning from India in July of 1979, I began to read Frits Staal's book, *Exploring Mysticism* (1975). In the following January, I wrote in my journal:

I've been considering some of the ideas of Frits Staal in *Exploring Mysticism*. He explains how past methods of studying mysticism have been insufficient. Mysticism needs to be studied from within, not from speculation. The student needs experiential and subjective data, which come only from the mystical experience itself. Thus the student should meditate following the instruction of a guru. However, analysis and critical judgment would disturb the meditation and the student's observations. The student should therefore observe and be receptive, but postpone any critical judgment.

In the Upanishads we find mentioned the four states of consciousness—being awake, dreaming, dreamless sleep, and the fourth, which is the experience of ultimate reality, the mystical state. The only difference between deep sleep and the mystical [fourth] state is one of awareness of one's state. [This is only one view, but it is the view that Staal left with me.] Staal believes that this identification between

dreamless sleep and mystical experience should be taken
seriously, and "may indeed provide a key to the understanding of mysticism" [Staal, 1975, p. 152]. Awareness is
essential to the study of mysticism. Although the person
asleep is not [normally] aware he is asleep, at least the
mystic is aware of his experience, and thus may study
mysticism from within.

I have not studied dreamless sleep from within, but
dreams. I also must suspend judgment until after the
dream, because judgment is not valid while dreaming...
Would perhaps critical judgment be impossible in the
mystical state as it is impossible in dreams?... Dreams are
not mystical experiences, but I have shut my eyes while
dreaming and had the dream environment disappear. Can I
eliminate, while dreaming, the dream environment and the
unconscious influence? Can I thus take my consciousness
into dreamless sleep, remaining aware of the experience?
Would I thus be in a mystical state? It certainly should be
easier to reach that state from a dream, where real bodily
awareness is already erased and the [dreamed] environment is more disposable.

If there is such a state as dreamless sleep, I wondered, what is it
like? After finishing other experiments, I decided I would try to
eliminate dream imagery when I realized I was dreaming to
see whether I could achieve anything that might be called
dreamless sleep. I had not come across any Hindu text that
discussed a possible procedure for moving from dream to
dreamless sleep. I was on my own and had no guru. I had no
goal beyond dreamless sleep. I could not even imagine what
dreamless sleep might be like, and I suspected that my
attempts would not lead very far. I regarded my intention to
find out what I could as just another experiment with dreams. I
did not think of this as a religious quest.

My journal entry for November 15, 1980, in which I wrote about my plan to investigate dreamless sleep, includes this paragraph:

> It is very noticeable how little my theological beliefs, the stories of the Bible, what I preach about sometimes with passion, and my calling as a Christian missionary enter into my dreams in any very obvious way. This is not the place to conjecture why. But as far as I can see, during sleep, it is in the elements of a dream that the influence of my religion could appear, and not in a state in which all elements of the dream are presumably eradicated.

Of course I was only conjecturing, and what I thought did not turn out to be correct. I figure now that my decision to try to create dreamless sleep was the point at which my dreaming started to become a spiritual journey, although I couldn't know it then. This journey I now think of as my pilgrimage into dreamless sleep.

To create dreamless sleep, I expected that I would need to eliminate all visual imagery and, in fact, all subjective experience of any kind, including body experience, while remaining asleep. Eliminating all experience proved to be difficult, which was no surprise. I will describe one of the first dreams in my attempts to eliminate dreaming.

> (November 17, 1980) I was sitting at a restaurant table with Charlotte, when I realized I was dreaming. There was a woman at another table, and I thought at first of doing some kind of experiment on her, such as passing my hand through her. Then I remembered what I was to do. I closed my eyes and saw darkness. Thus my visual dream imagery was quickly removed. My body experience remained the same—as though I was sitting in a chair in a restaurant, with my feet on the floor and leaning on the table with my eyes closed. I pushed the table away to eliminate awareness

of it. Then I raised my feet off the floor. I was still aware of
my body and of the chair holding me up. I was not sure that
I wanted to push away the chair that held me up. I
managed to will it away, and I remained in the air leaning
back with my legs raised. As I was no longer aware of the
chair, I began to float. Then I began to spin a little. Then
Charlotte came along and said that she thought we should
leave. So I got out of the chair and we left the restaurant.

7. Falling to the Light

After I decided to try to create dreamless sleep, I often did not
remember while dreaming that eliminating the elements of the
dream was my goal. And light, not thought about and
uninvited, soon began to play a part. A dream that preceded
my first experience of the fullness of light seems to have played
a role in the coming of the first fullness. My journal entry of
November 25, 1980, records:

> I was leaning over, but I was not in, a high bed. On the wall,
> above the head of the bed, was a small sign which said, in
> effect, that if I would fall out of bed, I would be at "the core
> of sunlight." I was aware that I was dreaming. This
> message was the promise of some grand experience if I
> would let myself fall out of bed. The words and meaning of
> the sign were actually more assumed than read word for
> word. I felt that this sign implied that, by falling, I would
> make a discovery.
>
> However, I didn't like the idea of falling, and I believed it
> would wake me up. I did not let myself fall and I woke up.

I did not make much of this dream. However, about two
months later, falling did become a part of my first experience of
the fullness of light. That event was brief and happened on
January 28, 1981. I was still trying to create dreamless sleep.

I was in front of my childhood home on Holly Place in Bellmawr Park. I wanted to show some people a high jump. When I jumped up above the people, I saw the top of my two-story brick home rise with me. So I realized I was dreaming. I descended and then began to fall. I believed by now that I could fall in a dream without fear. I did not expect to hit the ground. When I decided to stop falling, I straightened up and thereupon was back on the ground and near people.

Then I was in the air again. I remembered to close my (dreamed) eyes to eliminate visual imagery. I floated and gathered my knees into my arms. Then, although I had closed my eyes, I saw an intense white light on the periphery of my vision to my left and remembered that an appearance of light did not necessarily mean that the light in my bedroom was waking me up (as I had thought in earlier dreams). Then the light increased and intense light surrounded me. I was floating in light and spontaneously called "Father," meaning God. I woke up.

Upon waking reflection, I recognized that the event had some characteristics of mystical experience, but it did not occur to me that it might have been what it seemed to be, an actual encounter with God. I analyzed the whole experience in terms of dreaming, not of mysticism. In fact, in my journal, I recorded two breakthroughs—that I could now fall in a lucid dream without fear of crashing and that I could become aware of a strong light in a lucid dream without concluding that the light in my bedroom was waking me up. I did not recognize the true breakthrough, which was the first appearance of the fullness of light. After that, falling did not continue to be a prelude to the fullness of light. This dream of falling to the light marked the first sign of my spiritual progress in dreaming.

The day after I recorded that experience of light, a fellow student at the University of Pennsylvania, to whom I had mentioned my lucid dreams, loaned me her copy of Scott Sparrow's *Lucid Dreaming: Dawning of the Clear Light* (1976). Sparrow describes different experiences of light in his lucid dreams and presents lucid dreams as a doorway to spiritual experience, with emphasis on the appearance of light. This was the first I read of the association of light with lucid dreaming, although I had already seen light in lucid dreams in a variety of ways, including now my first fullness of light. Therefore, I could see a confirmation of my own experiences of light. However, Sparrow presented the experience of light as more mystical than I was then ready to accept.

From reading Sparrow's book, I also learned that lucid dreaming was an important part of some Tibetan Buddhist practices and that light played a part in Tibetan discussions of lucid dreaming. I had not yet begun to read about Tibetan Buddhism's connection with lucid dreaming. Sparrow mentioned Evans-Wentz's *Tibetan Yoga and Secret Doctrines* (1958) which I proceeded to buy and read. Actually, there was very little literature on lucid dreaming at that time, and books on Tibetan practices during sleep and dreams were not as numerous or detailed as they have become since then. I was still satisfied to think of the fullness of light in terms of sleep and dreams, not mysticism.

On August 11, 1981, I wrote in my journal:

> In what manner am I to consider the light? I am investiga-
> ting dreamless sleep because of its description in the
> Upanishads. In the Upanishads, I find two helpful verses. In
> *Praśna Upaniṣad* 4.6, we have, "When he is overcome by
> glory (*tejas*), then that faculty sees no dreams, and that
> [well-known] happiness arises in the body" [Zaehner,
> 1966]. *Tejas*, which Zaehner translates as "glory," is
> translated "brilliance" by Hume [1949], and "light" by
> Radhakrishnan [1953], Nikhilananda [1963], and Müller
> [1969]. When the dreamer is overcome by light, he sees no

dreams. Here the light is associated with the coming of dreamless sleep. What is the light? In *Mundaka Upaniṣad* 2.2.10 we find (Zaehner translation),

"In the highest golden sheath
Is spotless Brahman, whole,
Resplendent, light of lights:
Who knows the Self, knows it!"

There are problematical references to the light in the Upanishads, with the constant question of what is intended metaphorically and what literally. But this verse is insistent that *brahman* is light. When dreams disappear, the light of *brahman* comes. If I were proceeding as a Hindu I could approach the experience of light with this understanding.

However, I am a Christian. If I had begun these experiences in a devotional manner, particularly if I had approached the experiences through meditation rather than dreams, my Christian theological background could have given me expectations and explanations. My Quaker ancestors believed in the Inner Light, who is Christ, the inward experience of God's presence. The Inner Light will convince you of sin and will lead you on if you but wait for its leading. The basis of this conviction is the first chapter of the Gospel of John: "The true light, which enlightens everyone, was coming into the world." [John 1:9]

The references to Christ are clear. And Christ to me is the light of the world. But where does the metaphorical leave off and the literal begin? It is difficult for me to see any literal reference to the light of Christ. Christ as metaphorical light is sufficient for me. To me, the experience of light by Christian mystics is more supportive of a literal light than are the verses about Christ as light...

My approach to dream experiments from the beginning was to not assume answers, but to experiment and see what happens. Particularly at the beginning I had no reason to think of theology. Now I have had to think of theology, but see no reason to proceed any differently. It is most valuable if I proceed with no theological presumptions. This is possible, because although I truly have theological beliefs about the interior quest, I just as truly do not find my experience yet a matter of theology.

8. Stars

I found a wide variety of forms and intensities of light during lucid dreaming, and light appeared in a variety of contexts. One variety can appropriately be called stars.

(March 5, 1981) I stayed a long time at the beach, then found myself under the boardwalk. The nails coming down through the boardwalk were slightly above my head. I walked out from under the boards and the scene was quite changed, and with this I knew I was dreaming. I jumped into the air, which was now dark. There followed a long and most enjoyable flight through space.

I did not propel myself. I was tumbled about with great speed. I traveled huge distances in the darkness—this direction, then that direction—with my clothes flapping in the air. The wind was constant and swift against me. Bright stars appeared. I was tossed toward the stars. First I saw one area of stars and then I saw another, and I could not center my attention on anything. I continued sailing through space and never became still. Once I thought I might be seeing light at a distance.

I considered this dream to have been the most intense experience of "ecstasy," as I used the word then, that I had ever known. As I was tossed about, I had no memories and was aware of no context except the universe of stars within darkness. There was the thrill of intense movement as on a swing or a roller coaster, but with much greater distances. The "space travel" was out of my control and intensely exhilarating.

I now choose to use the word "euphoria" where formerly I used "ecstasy," because of the technical meaning of "ecstasy" as used in the study of religions. In ecstasy, the mystic (or shaman or ascetic), through contemplation, trance, dance, or other means, is carried beyond awareness of the external world. It is as though he or she has left the physical body behind. The loss of awareness of the physical body is the ecstasy. Any emotion or pleasure in the experience is not what is meant by the word. Mircea Eliade, for example, speaks of "the shamanic technique of ecstasy," meaning that the shaman "specializes in a trance during which his soul is believed to leave his body and ascend to the sky or descend to the under-world" (Eliade, 1964, p. 5).

I had already lost awareness of the external world and of my body upon falling asleep and beginning to dream, so my passage from ordinary dreaming or lucid dreaming to euphoric experience is not the coming of ecstasy in the shamanic sense. However, I would think that a shaman might have thought of my sky travel as ecstasy in the shamanic sense.

I have experienced two principal forms of euphoria during sleep. The present dream is an example of kinesthetic euphoria —an excitation and intensification of emotion arising from extreme bodily movement, as from riding on a roller coaster. Kinesthetic euphoria is in contrast to the experience of the full-ness of light, which is a devotional euphoria. With kinesthetic euphoria, bodily feelings are enhanced so that I am exhilarated. I may even call upon God or Christ, but I worship more because of my memory of intending to do so than by my worship being beyond my control. Sometimes I experience kinesthetic euphoria along with a visual field full of stars or even full of light, but the light as a whole does not have the intensity of the fullness of light, and the experience is neither religious nor numinous in the sense that the fullness of light is.

In contrast, in the fullness of light, such as in my "Amazing Grace" experience, joy and devotion are spontaneous and uncontrollable. The fullness is more numinous than physically exhilarating. Body experience tends to calm down rather than be exhilarating. In fact, body experience tends to become gradually lost as I give my attention to the light and God. Kinesthetic euphoria and the fullness of light, for me, are alternative possible developments. I have not experienced them on the same occasion. Nor has one developed from the other. Other writers, for example Patricia Garfield (1979), describe sexual "ecstasy" during lucid dreaming. This is outside my experience.

I still have a memory from when I was a child sleeping in my bedroom. I had such a dream as I told here, of shooting off at great speed among the stars for a very long time. When I woke up, I reflected that it was not at all like a dream. It seemed so real. But I knew no alternative to its having been a dream.

9. Uphill

In my attempts to create dreamless sleep, I thought of my goal as the elimination of dreaming. How dreaming was to be defined was not so clear to me at the time. I soon saw the most difficult part of my work as being the elimination of my dreamed body awareness. I feel that the dream on August 12, 1981, was the time I most thoroughly achieved the elimination of the dream.

> I was in a tribal area of northeast India resembling Nagaland or the Garo Hills. I was at the bottom of a hill. There were many young men about, some wrapped in tribal shawls. I saw the school buildings up on the higher part of the hill. The most impressive construction was a long, narrow platform made of bamboo and thatch extending from the front of the schoolhouse out over the side of the hill. The platform was marvelous, about 250 feet long and ten feet wide. It was covered by thatch and held up by a construction of long bamboo poles tied together.

I walked up the hill among the students, who were carrying books. At the top of the hill, I came to the entrance of the platform that extended out over the mountainside. The entrance was covered by drapes, which someone pulled back so that I and the man who was showing me around could walk out on it. I was surprised to see more students sitting out on the platform studying. They looked up at us. Then classes were to start, so the students left for the school building. It occurred to me that the missionary might have had the platform built as a place to get away from busy school life once in a while. The scene seemed so unlikely that I realized I was dreaming.

At first, as often happens, the attraction to the dream was so strong that I did not want to experiment. So we walked out toward the outer end of the platform. Eventually, I remembered my intention to eliminate as much of the dream as I could. So I obediently closed my eyes and created darkness. Then, according to a recent plan, I began to imagine a flame to concentrate on as I looked at the darkness. Soon, I saw a pale white spot in the darkness, which served as a flame for me, although it was not flame-like.

Eventually, my attention remained on the white spot very well. There were no distracting thoughts or circumstances. Then I felt my attention move out to the white spot and I lost awareness of my body. I'm not sure how to describe that movement. Then there was only darkness and then nothing. I did not wake up. When I did wake up, I had no memory of what immediately followed my disappearance in the darkness.

Afterward, I decided that it was through my concentration on the white spot that I forgot about and thus lost body imagery. That is the way dreams work. When I concentrate on one part of the imagery, my attention is withdrawn from other parts and

I tend to lose what I do not pay attention to. It is not that I concentrate on eliminating body imagery, for that would place emphasis on the body and make it difficult to eliminate.

I consider this case to be my best elimination of dreaming, but it came without my seeing intense light. I had eliminated all experience of any kind (such as memory, thought, or emotion), and also the darkness seemed to be eliminated, and I did not wake up. Since I did not remember what followed the elimination, I thought later that perhaps the forgotten period might even have been dreamless sleep, as I thought of it then. In any case, I was eventually left with no feeling that the event had been significant.

Another observation—about the pale white spot created through my imagining a flame. Several times, now, when I have begun to concentrate on an imaginary flame, a white spot has appeared, and has been for me a "flame" for concentration. As far as I am aware, never when I am awake do I ever, or can I ever, create a visual image, such as that "flame," through imagining, remembering, visualizing, daydreaming, desiring to, or trying to. I did not expect to create an image that I would see. For me, to imagine does not mean to literally see.

As I think about the matter now, years later, I realize that darkness would not need to disappear for the experience to be called dreamless sleep. That is, darkness itself cannot reasonably be called dream imagery. Darkness is the absence of imagery, at least in the way I use the word "imagery." However, the darkness would need to disappear if I were literally to create pure objectless consciousness, as the goal is for some Hindus, since darkness would be an object of consciousness. I was not yet taking into account the Tibetan concept of dreamless sleep according to the Naropa tradition, which I will deal with later.

10. A Disk of Light

In a dream of October 23, 1981, I was still trying to lose body imagery (to create dreamless sleep) by thinking of a flame to concentrate on.

> I was in the lower part of a tall, narrow university building, in an apartment on the ground floor, which was cut off from the upper floors. The rooms on this floor were lit up. To my right were stairs going down to the basement.
>
> I stepped clockwise down a spiral staircase into a small bright yellow apartment below ground level. There was a furnace burning in the curve of the stairs. Somehow I realized I was dreaming, and when I reached the floor below I closed my eyes and saw darkness. I began to think of a flame as I gave my attention to the darkness. I felt the floor under me at first, but as I concentrated on the darkness, I lost awareness of the floor and I rose up.
>
> As I continued to watch the darkness, I became aware of a disk of light to the left of my point of concentration in the darkness. As the top of me stayed still, my legs began to make a stirring motion in a circle like a spoon stirring, and I felt dizzy. Nevertheless, the disk of light stayed to the left of my area of concentration in the darkness. I did not think to shift my eyes or my attention to the disk itself. The disk of light stayed in the same location to the left of my point of concentration in the darkness even though I continued the stirring motion. After some time, I woke up.

On waking reflection, I estimated that the disk of light had appeared as if it were about ten inches in front of me, about three or four inches to the left of my point of concentration, and it had a diameter of about four inches. That is only the impression. I do not assume that such dimensions were literally involved nor that the light had appeared within some kind of three-dimensional space. The mention of dimensions is only a means of describing the figure. It never occurred to me to consider that there might be a connection between my trying to concentrate on an imagined flame and the appearance of the disk of light.

I should mention that when I concentrate on the darkness, I am usually not aware of any specific spot within the darkness that I can concentrate on. For the darkness all looks pretty much the same. For that reason, my attempt to concentrate on one point primarily takes the form of keeping my eyes absolutely still. In any case, since I kept my eyes still, I evidently did not scan the darkness or ever look directly at the disk.

As I analyzed the experience afterward, it did not occur to me that the disk of light might have had anything to do with dreamless sleep. I felt during this period that, in spite of the dream in which I disappeared at the top of the hill, I was not getting far with moving on to dreamless sleep. Although it did appear that my attempts to eliminate dream imagery were valuable to learn from, my goal of dreamless sleep continued to be elusive.

During these experiments and thereafter in other dreams, I saw various kinds of lights. The lights often appeared surrounded by darkness. Sometimes I saw darkness with no lights within it. The experiences of darkness were never numinous. Because I sometimes experienced darkness and sometimes saw a variety of lights, sometimes within dream imagery and sometimes within darkness, I began to wonder whether darkness or light would prove to be the way to dreamless sleep. I concluded that darkness was probably closer to dreamless sleep, since darkness seemed to indicate elimination more than did the presence of light.

11. A Prayer

When I began to read Teresa of Avila's *The Interior Castle* (1979),
I read that she advised the nuns to find someone with experience to help them understand the inner experiences that
accompanied their prayers. She advises that, if they don't find
someone, not to give up. The Lord will help. At the time I read
that, I was feeling continually alone in trying to understand my
experiences, which by then were becoming religious and
already included a couple of experiences of the fullness of light.
I had no guru or teacher to help me.

I then noted in my journal that, although I had no advisor
yet, I had come across some helpful teachers. At that time, I
could think of C.G. Jung, Frits Staal, S. Radhakrishnan,
R.C. Zaehner, Mircea Eliade, Steven Katz, A.R. Luria,
S.K. Saksena, R.D. Ranade, Sadhu Sundar Singh, Swami
Abhishiktananda, and many others. At the time, I was learning
a lot by comparing my own experiences with what Teresa, my
latest teacher, had to say.

In May of 1982, I wrote in my journal,

> I have found no one who could help me specifically in what
> I have been doing. I have not consciously taken my dream
> experiments before the Lord for help, because my motiva-
> tion has not been to have a religious or mystical experience.
> I have wanted to objectively find out about the nature of
> dreams. Could prayer on this matter possibly change the
> results? Because my Lord answers prayer? Because by
> prayer I set my mind in certain directions? Because I would
> interpret my results in the light of my prayer? Would
> praying be a recognition that this is now a mystical search
> instead of dream experiments? If I did not pray, would that
> be a failure to tap the only source of success in such a matter
> as this?

These religious questions were rather heavy for me, and it was about this time that my quest for understanding dreams became more obviously part of a spiritual journey. As I thought about this, I composed the following prayer and wrote it in the back of my Bible. For years after, I prepared myself for sleep by reading this:

> Lord, bless my dreaming, that I may become a better person and that I may know you better. Bless my dream experimenting, that I may learn more about dreams and dreamless sleep and whatever transcends them. Lead me into truth and not delusion. Lord, if it pleases you, let me have a taste of you. Lead me not into a cold objectivity that would close you out. Lead me not into a foolish subjectivity that would blind me to reality and truth. Lead me not into conclusions too clever. Keep me in the Way and the Truth and the Life. Amen.

12. Pushing the Bed Away

Although I had gotten into the habit for some time of trying to eliminate dream imagery to create dreamless sleep, the coming of the fullness of light appeared to happen spontaneously and did not appear to depend on my efforts to eliminate dream imagery. In the "Amazing Grace" dream, the fullness of light interrupted the ongoing dream. It did not come after the elimination of dream imagery. The light did, in fact, spontaneously replace all other visual imagery by filling the visual field. In seven of the thirteen cases of the fullness of light, the light appeared in the midst of my dreaming, without my giving any thought to the elimination of dream imagery. In two others, I had flown upward to eliminate dream content, before the light came, and once, the first time, I fell a distance and then closed my (dreamed) eyes before the fullness of light happened. Twice I had no memory of what had preceded the fullness of light.

That leaves this one experience (September 2, 1982), in which elimination was obviously a part of what led to the fullness.

Charlotte and I were moving back to the college in Jorhat, India, where we used to teach. As I carried furniture into our house, I reflected on my recent dreams of being back in India. But now I really was back. Or was I? No, of course not. I was dreaming. I remembered that I wanted to eliminate dream imagery. Actually, that had been an old plan. I had planned more recently, and did not remember, to just ignore the visual imagery instead of eliminating it and then think of God, repeating, "God is love."

Then I was kneeling over the side of a bed. A woman sat on the other side of the bed, and a man sat on the bed next to where I was kneeling. Intending to eliminate visual imagery, I placed my folded hands on the bed and closed my eyes to pray. Although I created darkness intentionally by closing my eyes, my praying was spontaneous and real. I began to repeat either "God is love" or perhaps "Praise the Lord."

I was aware of touching both the bed and the man next to me. As I prayed, I imagined pushing them away in order to eliminate them. I did not literally push. Then it was as though the feelings of touch moved away pulling me with them. But the feelings detached and I was left floating in darkness. I continued to praise God. Once I thought of repeating "Hallelujah," but remembered that that had not been my plan. It was not that I was entirely in control of what I was doing, but more that I was at the mercy of what I remembered. I began to repeat silently, "Blessed is the name of the Lord."

Then a brilliant white light appeared at the upper edge of the visual field, very slightly to the right of center, where it stayed for a moment. Soon a bright sun appeared a little lower but still high in front of me, where it remained for the rest of the experience. Intense, vibrant light filled my visual field. I was floating in light. I was aware of God and continued repeating joyfully, "Blessed is the name of the Lord."

By now, I had little or no awareness of the lower part of my body. I thought of my eyes as still shut in prayer. Any contradiction between thinking of my eyes as shut and seeing light didn't occur to me. I considered opening my eyes to see whether light was also around my feet, but I was too reluctant to interfere with the experience. Despite a few thoughts on what to do next, I remained intensely worshipful. I felt only slight involuntary movement, which was all that was left of body imagery. I continued repeating silently, "Blessed is the name of the Lord," until I remembered the text I had more recently planned (while awake) to say, "God is love," which I then repeated silently until I woke up.

When the light appeared, my attention remained visually on the light and mentally on God, with no thought of body imagery. What was left was the sun-like disk within an intense brightness that filled the visual field, minimal body awareness, knowledge of the presence of God, extreme joy, and a silent repeating of devotional phrases. Before the light, I had caused a gradual elimination of dream imagery.

What was left of my body image was the last element of my dreaming to go. It may even be that, because I was still seeing light, I assumed a body with eyes was still there to do the seeing, but it need not have been. The intense light remained and I will explain later why I do not include the light as dream imagery. I did nothing specifically that I know of to bring about the light of the fullness.

13. A Thousand Suns

An experience recorded on October 26, 1982:

> I do not remember at all what led to my experiencing the fullness of light. Nor do I remember in what order events happened while I was seeing the light. I was neither thinking nor remembering very well. It seemed I had planned what I was to do when I saw the sun again like this, but I could remember nothing.
>
> As I happily saw the form of the sun within the surrounding light, I was drawn up off the ground toward it, and I floated. I watched the light for some time, being somewhat stirred around. There was a period when I was afraid that the light was leaving me because of something I had done, and I renewed my attention toward the sun and the intensity of my devotion.
>
> Then I was aware of the sun again, whose light throughout the visual field was all I could see. The disk of the sun itself was right above my head, remaining in a position where I had to turn my eyes up to see it more directly. These words came to me, "When I before a thousand suns bring forth …" But I woke up before I could continue, and I felt a nervous tingling throughout my body.

In my journal afterward, I observed that I had not thought through the line about the thousand suns. It just came to me much the same way that lines of poetry had come to me several years before when I was experimenting with composing poetry during lucid dreams. In those dream experiments, I would stop whatever I was doing when I remembered to do so and passively let a couple of lines (hopefully) of poetry come to me. Never more than two lines came to me at a time. In the present dream, I anticipated more words coming except that I woke up. As in all the earlier experiments with poetry, what came to mind had a relationship to the ongoing circumstances of the dream. In this case, the words that came to me certainly were related to the fullness of light, for every part of the visual field was shining with the vibrant intensity that I see only when I look toward the sun while I am awake.

The expression "a thousand suns," however, most likely did not emerge freshly manufactured out of my unconscious processes, because sometime in the past I would have read the phrase "a thousand suns," in English translations and in Sanskrit, in the *Bhagavad Gita*. The relevant words are found in chapter 11, verse 12, upon the occasion of the god Vishnu revealing himself to Arjuna in his supreme form. The description of Vishnu goes like this:

> If the brightness of a thousand suns
> appeared in the sky all at once,
> that would be like the brightness
> of the great Self [meaning Vishnu].

This description of light was appropriate to my own circumstances and makes me think that "the brightness of a thousand suns" as described in the original Sanskrit verse was based on someone's personal experience.

It is also possible that some time before this dream I had read about Robert Oppenheimer's thoughts upon witnessing the first explosion of an atomic bomb in the American desert. The story is often told that Oppenheimer, who studied Sanskrit, recalled, upon seeing the explosion, this same verse from the *Bhagavad Gita* about the thousand suns.

14. Struggle

A few entries from my journal can give an idea of the struggle that I eventually felt about accepting the fullness of light as being what it seemed to be — an encounter with God.

November 10, 1982. For the past week I have felt bothered by the problem of the light. Today I have found the words that express what disturbs me. If the light is of God, this is an awesome and rare thing, and very important to me personally. If the light is not of God, this also is awesome, because many religious people have testified to the presence of the divine in the light for them, and they would be wrong. The magnitude of either possibility overwhelms me. And the fact that I don't know which awesome conclusion is correct disturbs me. My experience in the light has been for me in some manner an experience of God. The question is—in what manner? For the feeling that God has answered prayer or the singing of a hymn in church are also experiences of God in a manner, while not being direct physical experiences of God's presence. And I feel almost guilty for doubting the validity of my experiences in the light. While very happy to experience the light, I now have less desire to experiment with it, for I feel that diminishes what it can be to me. Certainly it is in some sense an experience of God. But am I only succumbing, as other people do, to my own theology? I am tossed back and forth with this problem.

February 16, 1983. A change has come about in my lucid dreams, particularly since the beginning of September. I see the fullness of light more frequently. When I do not see the fullness of light, I frequently feel that I am close to the experience. I stay lucid longer on the whole, to the extent that I forget some of what happens. I progress more quickly through the process that leads to the light. More is happening while I float, and these phenomena tend to be more non-realistic, imaginative, and awe-inspiring than what I normally dream.

June 21, 1983. The greatest struggle has been in deciding in what manner the experience in the light is an experience of God. I am pulled in opposite ways. My sleeping, irrational self accepts the experience as it happens as a meeting with God undoubtedly. It is an experience of God and it is self-authenticating. If I had not behind me years of analyzing my dream experiences, I would not have felt the need of stepping back while awake to look critically at the experience of light and analyze it away. So my rational self will say, "Yes, it is in some manner an experience of God," or "It is at the time an experience of God, but it is my unconscious that makes me feel it is so," or "I have in a sense experienced God, but if I analyze it, I see it is an experience of light, devotion, joy, and a feeling of God's presence, but not an experience of God." I must always qualify the statement and not leave it as an experience of God. Yet I can at the same time, while awake, look forward in hope that I may have the experience again, for then I am happiest and most aware of God, and worship more truly than any time when I am awake.

For years I have read and fed on Indian Christian literature that takes seriously the philosophical and devotional thoughts of the Upanishads, the Gita, the Yoga Sutras, the Vedanta schools, and their modern interpreters. These touch on many areas never approached by the Bible. But now I read Swami Abhishiktananda [the Benedictine monk] still devotionally and with appreciation, but when he speaks of the experience of the Self, the ego being consumed by the flame and the awareness of the Presence, I think, "I wish these precious ideas still meant to me what they used to, but though these experiences happen, they are not what they seem to be. They can be explained in terms of dream phenomena. There may be no ontological significance at all." Then I come back to myself with, "Do you really believe they mean nothing at all?" Well, no I don't. Unconsciously, I really believe. And so it goes. This has been my struggle for months now.

Don questioned me on the phone last night as to why I should give more weight to what my waking self thinks on the subject than to what I more instinctively believe.

And last night I had this nonlucid dream. I and another man were running clockwise around the outside of a large circular building. We kept pace with one another. But I had this idea that he should be running around it differently, perhaps through gardens and over porches at a distance from me. The significance was that, though we were supposedly running in two different manners, we were really together. I believe that the two were both myself … my two minds on the major question I have these days. Neither is ahead of the other, nor are they far apart.

June 23, 1983. I have avoided saying that in the light I actually experienced God. Until the last I have intended to explicitly deny this by including a sentence something like the following. "But just as when I experience Charlotte in a dream, it is not a direct perception of Charlotte, but an experience built upon and reflecting my real relationship to Charlotte, so this experience in the light is not a direct perception of God, but an experience built upon and reflecting my real relationship to God." My intuitive self knows that it is an experience of God. But my waking self, who is writing this, wants to be more rational, critical, and careful. My waking self is however not necessarily more perceptive or correct. I know that if I were to say without qualification that I did experience God in the light, it would be a matter of faith. My intuitive self, even now, wants the final say in this matter, for I really know that in some manner I have had in the light an experience of God. It is the "in some manner" that my more rational self wants to hold onto. But I will say it now unconditionally. I have experienced God in the light.

[I wrote this confession of faith two years and five months after the first fullness of light.]

15. Dream Worship

Before I fully accepted the fullness of light as an authentic experience of God, my approach to lucid dreaming was primarily to study the nature of dreams. When I was trying to eliminate the elements of dreaming while staying asleep, the religious experiences that arose in my dreams were unplanned and largely spontaneous. I appreciated them, but did not yet consciously think of my dreaming as a spiritual journey. In 1983, after I accepted my experiences of the fullness of light to be authentic experiences of the presence of God, my attitude toward dreams became more overtly religious. Worshiping while dreaming became more attractive to me than experimenting with dreamless sleep.

A dream of October 7, 1984:

> I was in India. I was lucid for so long, I have no memory of what led to knowing I was dreaming. I remembered my desire to praise God. I thought spontaneously to run in a circle singing hymns. I hesitatingly began to run counterclockwise in a large circle, trying to recall what the symbolic difference was between running clockwise and counterclockwise according to Jung. I couldn't think that through, and I kept running, dancing, and singing in the direction I had started. No particular thing marked the center to my circling.
>
> My running was quick, but not as though I were racing. I danced as I ran, with my arms moving to the music. I danced to the hymns I sang. Occasionally I spun around in little circles within the big circle, bearing to my left continually. I ran through fields, over rough ground, through people's yards enclosed within bamboo fences, by an old man sitting in his yard, and into and out of rooms and houses. The areas through which I ran and danced changed continually with no consistency. Generally I tried not to bump into things, but I also knew that I could simply

ignore anything in the way and pass through it, which I sometimes did. For a while, some playful children ran behind me. I thought that they might get in my way, and they partly took my mind away from my concentration on hymn-singing. However, I speeded up, and that too passed.

I may have sung ten different hymns one after the other. I probably did not sing more than one verse of each. Occasionally some words did not come to me and I easily put in my own words. There were pauses between the hymns while I thought of what to sing next. It seems to me I sang "Grace That is Greater Than All My Sins," at least the chorus. I know that I sang "Stand Up, Stand Up for Jesus." I had a momentary hesitation with that one, thinking that I wasn't standing up, but running and dancing in a circle. I thought of singing "Silent Night" since I had already sung a Christmas one (I forget which). I decided against "Silent Night" because it did not seem quick enough for my running and dancing movements. I believe I sang "Wonderful Words of Life." I might have sung "I Serve a Risen Savior." I know that I finished with "Jesus Loves Me," still moving counter-clockwise, after which I woke up. All the hymns, as often happens when I sing in my dreams, reached back to the years before I went to seminary in 1955.

No matter how much one believes in and enjoys communal worship, sleep forces us to be alone. But in our aloneness, we sometimes have others born from ourselves, other parts of ourselves, who will step into our dreams, and we can sing with them. Mostly I do the singing, but sometimes others decide what to sing. Above all, I still have a loving God with me in my dreams to worship and enjoy. Hidden behind the colors, forms, and sounds of our images, God waits to be invited into our song and dance. I will never see God, but God will be with me.

Dream worship has depended normally on my being lucid, and I have thought of doing so only occasionally. Much of my worship doesn't go far beyond singing hymns, dancing, and calling out scripture verses. Dancing is spontaneous and easy, although I have rarely danced with anyone or by myself when awake. I am not a dancer. In dreams, I also call out, even shout, little pieces of scripture or religious phrases, such as "God is love" or "Come, Lord Jesus."

I may also turn to the quieter and less exciting kind of worship that sometimes accompanies the elimination of dream imagery. I may float or concentrate on the darkness, and, without excitement, call on God. I have worshiped in a variety of dream circumstances, and there is no reason to believe that I have exhausted the possibilities.

Knowing that I am dreaming, I can make worship choices in some limited way and plan what to do next. However, my lucidity is balanced by the fact that I never have the degree of mental ability that some others claim to have in lucid dreaming. In dream worship, there is a certain advantage in having limited contact with the world and limited memory.

Most of us, when we pray while awake, close our eyes to minimize visual distractions. In meditation and contemplation, we may reach more deeply into ourselves, avoiding the distractions of the world. When I dream, I have reached a much higher level of eliminating distractions, and in lucid dreams, I also find fewer entanglements to distract me than I find in ordinary dreams or in being awake.

As in any dream, when I worship, my attention largely focuses on one thing at a time. I am not disturbed by the worldly concerns of my waking life. There are for me only the contents of the dream. In dream worship, God is the essential part of the experience and usually has my complete attention. I worship God and am centered on what I am doing. The usual narrow focus of my attention in dreams helps as well in the quieter attempts at stillness and concentration as well as in the more active worship.

Forgetting my past and the rest of the world means also that my worship, for better or worse, is not affected by clergy, religious surroundings, other worshipers, liturgy, hymn books, the way things are usually done in church, or whether I should be sitting or standing. I cannot even pray spontaneously about a waking life that I can only vaguely remember. My singing, calling verses, and praising God largely become my prayers. Worship comes from deep within me. My deepest religious impulses are released. I sing what I have learned long ago, although I can supply new words when I have forgotten some.

There is something in me that wants to worship God. Something in me chooses the hymns — something at work among my memories. I will sometimes be at the mercy of remembering a plan that I had made while awake, but largely I worship spontaneously and joyfully, without waking inhibitions. I do not think things through very far. My source is in my religious history, what I am, and what I truly believe. And as Paul wrote, "It is God who is at work in you, enabling you both to will and to work for his good pleasure" (Phil. 2:13), so that the spirit of God works within what I am. In dream worship I am alone with God, and I am at the mercy of God and myself. My worship is honest. Even when I worship because I remember some waking plan to do so, I worship truly and with little artifice. I seem incapable of pretense.

As Jesus taught the Samaritan woman, "God is spirit, and those who worship him must worship in spirit and truth" (John 4:24). It seems to me that dream worship meets that ideal more easily than worship while awake, at least for me. I believe that such worshiping in spirit must be a blessing and balm to the body and mind asleep in bed.

16. Bless the Lord, O My Soul

Two entries from my journal:

June 27, 1990. "Bless the Lord, O my soul; and all that is within me, bless his holy name" (Ps. 103:1). Surely as I praise or bless the Lord as I dream, my very soul blesses the Lord. And how wonderful if all I am will praise the Lord. As I dream, all that I dream is of myself. All that appears in the dream is mine and is all that is within me. How wonderful if every part of me will praise the Lord. This is how I want to bless the Lord when I am lucid in a dream — through all that is within me — every piece of earth, tree, house, and all people in the dream. I must try to remember this verse for when I dream lucidly. I do know how to sing it. How better to get all that is within me to bless his holy name.

March 26, 1991. I was in Jorhat a very long time. There was something that we were to do with the police. I heard my name called, so I knew they [the police] were expecting me and it should be all right. I went into a room to talk to the officials. I thought in there I might speak Assamese and surprise them, but we spoke English. I was then wandering through the building, realizing I was dreaming, but ignoring the fact. I remembered that there was something I wanted to do. I didn't think of it right away.

Then I remembered, "Bless the Lord." I began to sing it loudly. Then I remembered I wanted other people to join in. I looked into a room and suggested we all sing "Bless the Lord." Then we all sang it and I reflected that all the people within me (in the dream) were singing it. We kept singing it all the way through — "Bless the Lord, O my soul, and all that is within me, bless his holy name." The people in the room had stood up at my suggestion and had sung it heartily, as I had.

I then recalled that I wanted everything in the dream to sing. I looked down an empty hall. The paint was peeling all over. I suggested to the hall that we all sing. I thought the hall could sing by using peeling paint for mouths. Then

I started to sing again with the hallway and the sound of the other voices changed, supposedly from people voices to hall voices. The singing reverberated in the hallway. We sang the verse again, maybe once or twice, and I woke up.

17. Come, Lord Jesus

I realized that for some time my dream experiences were obviously very much God-centered rather than Christ-centered. That was fine and that is the form my unplanned worship took. However, being puzzled by that, I planned to look for an experience of Christ when I knew I was dreaming. Here are excerpts from my journal that tell about my attempts at that time.

April 5, 1985. Most nights as I set about to go to sleep I repeat to myself something like the following — "I am going to sleep. I will dream. I will realize I am dreaming and then I will praise Christ." Then I suggest to myself that in the dream I may praise Christ by singing the hymn, "All Hail the Power of Jesus' Name" [tune: Coronation]. I then repeat or sing these words mentally to myself as I go to sleep and also say the words, "Come, Lord Jesus."

August 19, 1985. Looking beyond Manhattan, I saw a long range of high mountains. I felt that there should not be a range of mountains there and then realized I was dreaming. I wondered at first what to do. Fortunately, I remembered that I wanted to praise Christ. I stood on the side of a mountain and happily looked into the sky [perhaps by habit, from old attempts to eliminate visual imagery]. I raised my arms and called, "Praise Christ. Praise Christ." I then went on shouting a series of other praises which I don't remember.

I lost awareness of the ground and found I was floating in the sky in an upright position, with my arms raised. Suddenly I remembered to sing. I sang "All hail the power

of Jesus' name, let angels prostrate fall." I sang not too
loudly at first. Then I remembered that it doesn't matter
how loudly I sing when I'm dreaming and increased my
volume. I sang through the line, "Bring forth the royal
diadem and crown him Lord of all," but woke up before
repeating that line as the last line.

I have come further along in this project. I still did not
remember the goal of what I was doing—symbolized in the
phrase "Come, Lord Jesus."

January 3, 1986. I realized from my flying that I was
dreaming. My first impulse was to go on with the dream.
Then I remembered that I wanted to see Christ, and decided
I would go ahead and attempt to do that. The scene was still
somewhat dark. I landed back on the ground, stood there,
and looked before me thinking of my Lord, whom I wanted
to see. For a moment I thought it might be too dark for
looking for him.

I felt a little pinch on the back of my right calf. My first
impulse was to swish away with my hand whoever was
bothering me back there. But then a better instinct,
accompanied by a vague memory that disturbances in a
dream are not easily disposed of, led me to swoop down
and take into my hands what turned out to be a child that
had touched me. I held the child, perhaps between the ages
of one and two, very lovingly, and the boy put his arms
around my neck. I knew that this was what I should do,
that this was perhaps even the way I was to find Christ in a
dream. It felt a little like the child's pants were wet, but that
did not matter. Being affectionate with the child was more
important.

The boy leaned toward my ear and said, "Finished
everything." And I knew that this was a lovely way for my
search for Christ to finish—to find him in others. So I
understood and agreed, and said to the child, "Shall I go?"

since it was then finished. And he answered, "Yes." So, I walked away carrying him. Then I woke up.

The Scripture says of Jesus,

"Then he took a little child and put it among them; and taking it in his arms, he said to them, 'Whoever welcomes one such child in my name welcomes me and whoever welcomes me welcomes not me but the one who sent me'" (Mark 9:36–37).

18. In the Spirit

In the book of Revelation, John begins his narrative of seeing the visions that came to him on the island of Patmos by saying, "I was in the spirit on the Lord's day, and I heard behind me a loud voice like a trumpet saying 'Write in a book what you see' …" (Revelation 1:10–11a). Angels speak to John and show him many things. An angel, speaking to John like a trumpet, said, "Come up here, and I will show you what must take place after this" (4:1b). At once he was in the spirit. Later, one of the angels carries John away "in the spirit" to a great high mountain and shows him the holy city Jerusalem coming down out of heaven from God (21:10). On February 28, 1989, I wrote in my journal the following:

> I spent some time in the night, what I thought of as "being in the Spirit." The phrase comes from Rev. 1:10, in which John says, "I was in the Spirit on the Lord's day." John then proceeds to tell of his visions. In this experience, I spent some time with a great multitude of people, or at least spiritual beings. I was not clear about their status and did not think about it. There was no ground to stand on, nor were there buildings or any visual environment other than the other beings who were also in the Spirit. Everything was done in the air. I specifically thought of my state as "being in the Spirit." Most of the time I spent with the others praising God. I do not remember a lot of what I said,

but I said once, while dipping up and down in the air, "It is wonderful to be in the Spirit praising God."

I did not see light. In fact, I did not even see the other people very well. I didn't even pay much attention to the other people. I guess I would say it was not very well lit. But it was a religious experience of flying, or at least of floating, with other people, all the time praising God. There was a brief time when I flew with my left arm over the shoulders of another, a male, with his arm over my shoulders, as we went up and down in the air in unison, praising God.

I have not yet referred to this as a dream. Surely I dreamed it. But this was more to be compared with mystical ecstasy or out-of-body experience. Dreamed, yes, but far from any ordinary dream. Not even a lucid dream, as such, and I will not count it as a lucid dream. During the experience, I never thought of it as a dream. However, I was aware that I was not awake, for I knew that I was "in the Spirit."

This night's religious experience has shown me the possibility that being in the Spirit is quite obtainable apart from lucid dreaming. I also believe that this is what "being in the Spirit" may mean in the Bible—religious experience in which one is aware that one is neither awake nor dreaming—that is, one is lucid, but it is not like dreaming. Last night was more different from dreaming than even lucid dreaming is different from ordinary dreaming. It was a joyful time of freedom and worship. It was basically and only a religious experience, a time of prayer and praise.

I do not imply that what I saw and did in the night is anything like what John records in his Revelation. Not at all. There must be countless paths into, within, and through that sacred place where one worships God. God may even come to meet us before we know what is happening.

19. An Ordinary Dream

Ordinary dreams are also gifts that I must appreciate. By "ordinary dreams," I simply mean dreams in which I do not realize I am dreaming.

(About August 8, 2002) I was with Indian Christians in Assam. The city seemed like Gauhati [Gauhati, now renamed Guwahati, was our home for eleven of our twenty years living in India]. We toured the Christian properties, possibly the hospital and office grounds. Someone heard that there was to be a Kali Agri somewhere nearby. Kali is a Hindu goddess. No meaning of Agri (ah-gree) comes to mind. It meant to me that there was to be some kind of ceremony — in this case related to Kali. Sometimes I went to see Hindu ceremonies out of curiosity, so we walked downhill toward the river (the Brahmaputra) to see it.

We stopped to watch a Hindu holy man (sadhu) sitting on a large cloth on the ground near the river. We sat around him on the sand of the riverbank. He had a number of items scattered across his blanket. He was old, with matted long gray hair. He was pleasant and looked at us. He held up a small brass tray holding a few ceremonial items. I thought I would put five dollars on the tray, not as an offering to Kali, because that was not my religion, but as a gift to him. I pulled out a huge wad of bills, but could not find a five dollar bill among them. He looked at me and commented on all the money I had — not in the sense of asking for money, but in the sense of making an observation about me.

Suddenly one of the Christians with me began to sing a familiar hymn, "I come to the garden alone, while the dew is still on the roses, and the voice I hear falling on my ear, the Son of God discloses ...," a commonly-known Christian hymn. My first reaction was to feel that singing the hymn was inappropriate in these circumstances. However, all the

Christians who were around me were then singing it, so I
joined in. I believe we sang the whole first verse, finishing
with "And he walks with me and he talks with me and he
tells me I am his own, and the joy we share as we tarry
there, none other has ever known." And then I woke up.

This nonlucid dream made me think a lot, because its meaning
for me was not immediately clear. I came to understand that
the dream was reminding me that at my innermost self I am a
Christian. It was showing me that no matter what friendliness
or understanding I have for the sadhu or for Hindus, it is
devotion to Christ that rules my center. It is that more inward,
deep devotion of mine that brought to life my singing Christian
friends. I found that I was singing that hymn off and on for the
rest of the day.

20. A Strange Sleep

When I planned my dream experiments around the concept of
dreamless sleep, I had no guide. Even though what I knew
about dreamless sleep was what I read in Hindu philosophy,
nothing I found in Hindu literature suggested how I could
move from dream sleep to sleep without dreams. Nor did I
know of any biblical or Christian literature that would give me
any insight into what I was trying to do.

I did have some understanding of what the Hindus believe
about the phenomenological and religious aspects of what I
was doing, at least in a broad, imprecise sense. The Hindu, and
later the Tibetan Buddhist, teachings gave me a way to think
about what was happening to me as a Christian pilgrim
traveling through the world of sleep and dreams. It seemed not
entirely an accident that my pilgrimage began while I was in
India and that the people I met along the way in books and in
this journey talked to me, in a manner of speaking, in Sanskrit
and (later) Tibetan. I don't at all understand why, but some
combination of what I am, what I did, my physical,

psychological, and religious history, and especially the hidden working of grace in me led to my experiences of light, and ultimately to the fullness of light.

I did not try to have lucid dreams. Lucid dreams came to me. Harry Hunt (1991) shows that there is something about lucid dreaming itself that helps to make my progress look like a natural development. In Hunt's analysis of lucid dreaming, he says,

> Lucid dreaming involves the attainment and maintenance of an attitude identical to that sought within the insight or mindfulness meditative traditions, especially as exemplified by Ch'an, Theravadean, and Tibetan Mahamudra Buddhism. Both insight meditation and stabilized lucid dreaming involve the development of a detached receptive (witness) set and its progressive balancing with the participatory involvements (doings) of everyday life. (1991, pp. 266–267)

> The strongest evidence for this equation of lucidity and meditative awareness comes from the prominence of lucid and control dreams within advanced Tibetan Buddhist practices—where lucidity is sought as the form of meditation available naturally during dreaming sleep. (*ibid.*, pp. 267–268)

I did not think of what I was doing as meditation or as something necessarily Hindu or Buddhist. After all, if there was such a state as dreamless sleep, it would no more be a Hindu state than dreaming is. In any case, Hunt's wording points out the Eastern connection with my spiritual development (see also Hunt, 1989). Nevertheless, I feel that all that happened with me and that led me to the light of the presence of God was in harmony with my Christian faith.

In fact, the Christian scriptures give us examples of God at work in dreams. I'll mention only a few examples, as plenty is already written about this matter (for example, Kelsey, 1974; Sanford, 1989). There is Jacob's dream at Bethel of a ladder reaching to Heaven, with angels ascending and descending on it, whereupon the Lord, the God of Abraham, promised to give Jacob and his offspring the land on which he was sleeping (Genesis 28:10–17). There is the promise from God to the prophet Joel that "I will pour out my spirit on all flesh; your sons and your daughters shall prophesy, your old men shall dream dreams, and your young men shall see visions" (Joel 2:28). In the Gospel of Matthew (1:20), the angel of the Lord appeared to Joseph in a dream and said that he should not be afraid to take Mary as his wife. In the same Gospel (2:12), the Magi were warned in a dream not to return to Jerusalem after meeting with the child Jesus. Religious visions of light are also recorded in the Bible. Well known among Christians is Saul's conversion on the road to Damascus (Acts 9:1–9) and the trans-figuration of Jesus on the mount (Matt. 17:1–8).

The relationship between mysticism and sleep and dreams has not been analyzed in Christian traditions to the extent that it has been in Indian traditions. I have pictured the Christian mystics deep in prayer or contemplation and, in this way, finding their way to unity with God. I believe also that occasionally Christian mystical experience has come sponta-neously, sometimes when one is awake, sometimes when one is asleep. However, I am assured that the great mystics of the Christian tradition were not total strangers to seeing sleep and dreams as playing a part in their religious experience.

Christian mystics occasionally have made note that parts of their mystical process, although presumably not normally approached through ordinary falling asleep, resembled sleep and dreams, but in a strange way.

Gregory of Nyssa writes about mystical experience:

> This is indeed a strange sleep and foreign to nature's custom. In natural sleep the sleeper is not wide awake, and

he who is wide awake is not sleeping. Sleeping and waking are contraries and they succeed and follow one another. But in this case there is a strange and contradictory fusion of opposites in the same state. For *I sleep and my heart watcheth.* (quoted in O'Brien, 1964, p. 48)

After lulling to sleep every bodily motion, it receives the vision of God in a divine wakefulness with pure and naked intuition. May we make ourselves worthy of this vision, achieving by this sleep the awakening of the soul! (*ibid.*, p. 49)

Teresa of Avila, in describing her progress through her "interior castle," compares two parts of this progression.

Don't think this union [the prayer of union] is some kind of dreamy state like the one I mentioned before. I say "dreamy state" because it seems that the soul is as though asleep; yet neither does it really think it is asleep nor does it feel awake. There is no need here to use any technique to suspend the mind since all the faculties are asleep in this state—and truly asleep—to the things of the world and to ourselves. As a matter of fact, during the time that the union lasts the soul is left as though without its senses, for it has no power to think even if it wants to. (Teresa of Avila, 1979, p. 86)

The author of *The Book of Privy Counseling* has likewise used the language of sleep to describe his spiritual work.

You, however, must not be afraid to commit yourself in radical dependence upon God or to abandon yourself to sleep in the blind contemplation of God as he is, far from the uproar of the wicked world, the deceitful fiend, and the weak flesh. …

It is not without reason that I liken this work to sleep. For in sleep the natural faculties cease from their work and the whole body takes its full rest, nourishing and renewing itself. Similarly, in this spiritual sleep, those restless spiritual faculties, Imagination and Reason, are securely bound and utterly emptied. Happy the spirit, then, for it is freed to sleep soundly and rest quietly in loving contemplation of God simply as he is, while the whole inner man is wonderfully nourished and renewed. (Johnston, 1973, p. 167)

While no teacher gave me a clear map to follow, I have by now compared notes with Paul the Apostle, Teresa of Avila, Symeon the New Theologian, the writer of *The Cloud of Unknowing*, the composers of the Upanishads, Patanjali (the historic teacher of yoga), Naropa and his Tibetan interpreters, and many others along the way, mostly to find insights and explanations of what was happening with me. I do not believe that what I write in this testimony gives anyone else a very clear map to follow either. This is more of a testimony to the incomparable joy and peace that comes from encountering God than it is a suggestion of how to plan such a pilgrimage. But I do believe that the most important ingredient in the preparation for and fulfillment of this pilgrimage is a love and desire for God.

It is true that some of my own religious experiences have happened within dreams, or at least within lucid dreams. However, I hope I make clear in this testimony that the fullness-of-light events are not simply dreams just because they happen during sleep. The fullness of light with the presence of God interrupts or breaks into the dream. While some dream elements may remain, such as dreamed body experience which may slowly disappear, the light itself, which overcomes all other imagery is not dream imagery, and the knowledge of the presence of God is not ordinary knowledge. Later, I will say more about such matters.

II

Near Death

21. Near Death

(February 18, 1985) In an ordinary dream, I was explaining to people about death. I was not thinking about my own death. The discussion was not simply theoretical. It was serious because of circumstances and possibilities that I cannot now remember. It was related to real possibilities. I said, "You will see both darkness and light at the same time," meaning that they would pass through the border between darkness and light and enter the light.

After a transition within the dream, which I have forgotten, I was floating in darkness wondering what was happening to me. I was aware of going through some kind of crisis that I did not understand. Although I was little aware of my body, I floated up. At first I did not think I was dying.

Suddenly I floated up out of darkness into intense white light, which I happily remembered from earlier occasions was the light of the presence of God. I understood that this time I was dying—that, in fact, I had died. The light was brilliant, seeming to radiate from a small bright sun in front of me slightly above the level of my eyes and filling the visual field. The light appeared to be whiter than usual. Rays extended from the sun. The sun was round, but almost like just a point of origin for the rays. Some rays started as tangent to the circumference of the sun and others radiated strictly from the sun's center.

I did not remember the circumstances of my death. I had some regrets about dying, but my resignation and acceptance were greater than any regrets. Besides, it was difficult to regret dying, since I could remember very little of my life. I knew I was in the presence of God and was spontaneously prayerful, calm, and very happy. While I floated in light, I repeatedly called, "Thank you, Father." I was not thanking for my dying, but for my being in the presence of God and the light. The enjoyment of the fellowship with God overcame any regrets.

After some time, I woke up gradually, not suddenly. I slowly became aware of my body lying in bed. I was tingling and very surprised to find that I was still in bed in Calcutta and not dead.

The coming of the fullness of light in this experience continued the themes of death, darkness, and light of the preceding dream. This time, darkness was an important precedent to the coming of light, but it was not like darkness that I have created at other times by closing my eyes.

I became lucid upon seeing the light instead of in a dream before the coming of light. Therefore, this is the only coming of the fullness of light that did not begin, strictly speaking, within a lucid dream. I did not realize I was dreaming, because I didn't believe I was dreaming. I believed I had died. But I knew that I was in the familiar presence of the light that I had experienced before.

What was the meaning of the near-death experience for me? Afterwards, I thought of four possibilities:

1. That I was really near death. The Tibetans explain that the clear light of the Void may be experienced not only during meditation, but upon dying. It is also well-known that near-death experiences related by those in the West who actually

were near death also most often include light. My experience is a variation of what others say about their being near death. However, to my knowledge, this experience did not occur due to any illness or to my being physically near death. When I woke up, I was not aware of any physical crisis.

2. That to be near God is to be near death. This may be true in some philosophical, psychological, theological, or technical meaning. However, none of my earlier experiences of the fullness of light have included any thought of death. Perhaps this time I was being shown a connection between the presence of God and death.

3. That the whole experience of dying was a metaphor for some serious change happening to me—a crisis of some sort that I cannot explain. This "near-death experience" was, as it turned out, the last of the thirteen experiences that I have called "the fullness of light." These experiences happened over a period of four years. This last one happened under very different circumstances from earlier ones. I was living alone in Calcutta, working on my doctoral dissertation in Sanskrit, and learning that, in spite of my enjoyment of India, I do not thrive so well apart from my family. I do not think that I was depressed, but loneliness and a few other practical factors that interfered with my work made me wonder, upon later reflection, whether such circumstances contributed to the "near-death" experience, meaning that it was a metaphor for my state of mind in that situation. In the end, I was not convinced that the near-death experience as a metaphor for the state of my mind would be enough explanation.

4. That the near-death part of the experience was simply a continuation from the earlier discussion about death in the preceding dream. However, I hesitate to consider the experience of the fullness of light to be simply the last part of the dream that preceded it. I think it more likely that the preceding dream discussion was a preparation for the near-death experience, whatever its meaning.

In any case, even though I am not sure how best to understand the near-death experience, I do not feel that its relationship to dreaming, as a continuation of the dream or as metaphor, diminishes its possible meaning or importance. In fact, for me, the relationship of the near-death experience to dreaming, instead of diminishing the importance of the near-death experience, raises the religious importance of dreams. Any fullness of light, by its context of sleeping and dreaming, suggests that sleep and dreams may be of more religious meaning and potential than is commonly thought.

Although I cannot explain it, there was something authentic about the experience that I have not been able to explain away by knowing that I woke up from it. I can wait to die, but I do see dying as very beautiful.

22. Goodness

The city of Varanasi (Banaras) is considered to be the holiest of Hindu religious centers. I was staying in Varanasi in early March 1985 for photographing a Sanskrit manuscript at Banaras Hindu University in relation to my dissertation work, which was the translation of a Sanskrit text on Hindu pilgrimage. My stay in India was coming to an end. I realized that I was becoming more obsessed with writing my discoveries about dreaming, visual imagery, and religious experiences of light than I was with completing my dissertation. I felt the increasing need, even an obligation, to think about and write about the kinds of visual experiences that I was coming to understand and which I write about in this account. The near-death experience had happened to me only a few weeks before traveling to Varanasi and was very much on my mind.

By now I had accepted the fullness of light to be a true awareness of the presence of God, but so far I had no one that I felt I could talk to very deeply about my experiences. During my stay in Varanasi I was visiting a few Roman Catholic priests or, more likely, brothers (I don't remember) at their compound. While we sat around outside informally, I hesitatingly told them about my experiences of the fullness of light. I had some hope that they might have something valuable to say to me.

Only one thing remains with me from this conversation. I cannot remember the exact words, but I can give the gist of what one of the men said. He said that experiences of God, such as I described and claimed to have had, may be judged to be authentic according to the goodness of the person having them. Goodness must be evident in a person's life or that person's "mystical" experience cannot be real. This was actually a worthwhile observation with a high potential for shutting me up.

After thinking of how to respond, I answered with more or less these words, "Well, concerning my goodness, that is a judgment others would have to make." I felt that whether I was a good person or bad or somewhere in between was not something I could say or even know. I could act humbly and say that I don't think I'm very good. But that would be just an expected pious statement. In fact, I don't really know how to rate my goodness.

The experience of the fullness of light is an act of grace, but how relevant is the experience to the question of goodness? If one must be good to merit the experience, how is it then an act of grace? How much better must one become afterward in order for the act of grace to be considered authentic? If I presume that God has some purpose behind this act of grace, what part must goodness play? I believe that God has worked in my life for a purpose, and as far as I can see, the purpose of the latter half of my life is to testify to and explain what I have discovered about how dreams and seeing happen, particularly what I have learned about seeing the fullness of light. I believe I have a testimony to give. I tend to think of the purpose of having these experiences, rather than of goodness. These thoughts were not part of my immediate response, but questions that I had to gradually think through.

23. Metaphor

For some years I questioned, what is the connection between God as metaphorical light (I John 1:5) and the literal experience of the fullness of light? I could not think of God as being light waves, or the source of light waves, or as a visual image of brightness. Even during the fullness I do not confuse the light of the fullness and God, who I feel is present.

Likewise, I could not accept that the experience of the fullness of light was simply expressing the metaphor of God as light. The fullness of light presented itself to me as an important event in itself rather than as a metaphor for something else. I felt that either I was experiencing a metaphor, as I do when I dream, or I was experiencing more than a metaphor —the presence of God. I believed the latter. So I was left with light as a metaphor for Christ or God and a literal experience of light, as in the fullness of light, without a clear connection between the two.

Dreams are known for their value as metaphors. Ernest Hartmann (1998) says that the noting of similarities is at the heart of metaphor, and that the showing of similarities probably occurs in every dream. The picture that the dream presents is a way of saying something true about my life. A metaphor explains. However, the light of the fullness with its sun is part of the experience of the presence of God, and not itself just a dream. That was the way I saw it.

Without negating this earlier thinking, I have come to appreciate the possibility of the fullness of light as metaphor. By "fullness of light," I mean the whole experience, all its content, beginning with the appearance of light until I wake up, not just the image of light itself.

It is clear that the fullness of light often shows its continuity from the flow of the dream that preceded it. A good example of this is in the "Amazing Grace" experience. Here, the fullness of light came as a fitting climax to the dream that led up to it. There was the continuity of subjective body imagery, thought, emotion, and religious feeling from the dream of the singing tea laborers to the appearance of intense light, and the preceding dream and the fullness of light formed one religious event. Whatever psychological, internal, or spiritual processes lay behind the dream appeared to lie also behind the appearance of light that followed it. Or at least the dream was the preparation for the coming of the fullness.

Another clear case is the "near death" experience. Although there was part of the dream that I forgot, the earlier discussion of death, darkness, and light in the dream preceded the "near death" experience of darkness and then light, with the overwhelming presence of God. The continuity from dream event to the fullness of light does not appear to be by chance.

When I see that the fullness of light is in continuity from the dream that precedes it, how can I assume that the possibility of metaphor-making has been cut off by the transition from dreaming to the experience of light? Perhaps the fullness of light is even an intensification of metaphor. What the metaphor is a metaphor for—that is, what the light as a metaphor corresponds to and explains—must lie beyond the phenomenon itself and somehow, you would think, be related to me. It must tell about something of ultimate importance in my life. The metaphor must tell something about my relationship with God, perhaps something that is beyond my understanding, something that may not be obvious to me.

I believe that the fullness of light as metaphor is not opposed to its being other things as well. Just as dreaming produces metaphors, experiences of the presence of God can produce the metaphor of brilliance. I believe that the fullness of light as metaphor does not in any way conflict with my understanding of the light as an important part of knowing the presence of God.

(This is as far as I got in this consideration of the light and metaphor.)

24. Walking Down Main Street

At the Moorestown church, Charlotte and I were at an evening book study of Parker Palmer's *Let Your Life Speak* (2000). The subject was about finding your vocation—doing something in life that you cannot not do. Charlotte told her story. I was reflecting on the fact that if I were to tell my story about leaving my doctoral program in Sanskrit to write what I had to write— the kind of things that I talk about in this book—I would be straying too close, perhaps, to my emotions. I was mentally involved in the discussion, but preferred to remain largely quiet.

That evening discussion seemed to be my preparation for the thought processes of the following day, May 20, 2010, as I took my walk along Main Street in Moorestown. The whole question of leaving my Ph.D. dissertation in order to write what I needed to write had been brought to the surface again for me. By now, much of my phenomenological writing had been published, but my manuscript, *A Testimony to Light*, now called *Seeing*, which had been around for years in various forms, with some sharing, some queries to publishers, and at least eleven rewritings, still had a thoroughly uncertain future. I think, how can I know that this is the work I am called to do and yet have its publication so much in doubt? How can I be writing for the religious public and people not know what to say to me as they try to read what I write? Are some of my observations really as important as I think they are? What kind of a testimony is my *A Testimony to Light* if it isn't read? How do I explain what I have been doing for the last 25 or so years?

So I was walking along Main Street, reviewing some of these thoughts, due to the book study the evening before, when I remembered my "near death" experience in February of 1985 in Calcutta. I suddenly saw what that experience was about— not just as knowing the presence of God, but as a wider metaphor. I had questioned the meaning of that experience for years, but had not pinned down an answer. I had also become willing to recognize the place of metaphor in the experience (see the section before this). I suddenly realized that the "near death" event was a metaphor that marked the crucial point in my turning from my years of Sanskrit studies to the writing of my phenomenological observations and especially, among them, the writing of my more religious manuscripts, particularly this testimony.

Although that dream plus fullness of light event in 1985 came to me as a near-death experience, I realized that the metaphor to be deciphered was not "near death." The metaphor was death followed by life. I was not wrong to believe I had died. The death metaphor captured my leaving (dying to) my years of focus on a doctoral degree, my dissertation, a career, and a future way of making a living, perhaps by teaching. I did not die to Sanskrit, for that has remained a part of my life. And the fullness of light itself was not like a death, but a most intense form of life after death. Light after darkness. It was not only a knowing of God's presence, but a metaphor for my rising to a focus on the living presence of God and on the writing to which I am called, which I cannot not do.

This interpretation finally feels right. The dream followed by light did in fact happen just at that hinge between doctoral study and having my own writing, the writing that came to me, take over my life. It appeared that God was being present for me right at the center of that transition. And the light became for me a metaphor for what was happening to me then and there. I now saw this, my last fullness of light, in a much broader context.

And this was not just a dream, although the "near death" began with a dream. This was a real event. The dream and the following light were also a metaphor, although for years I was not able to comprehend it. My discovering this broader meaning of the "near death" as I walked along Main Street strengthens my view that my decision was right, to do what I cannot not do, even if I don't know what will become of what I write.

This interpretation suggests that my earlier experiences of the fullness of light were also not just isolated other-worldly events, but that they came to me in the context of what was happening within me day after day while I was awake and while I was asleep.

III

Image

---

25. Lattices

My pilgrimage into dreamless sleep had many stops, byways, and detours, and now I must take you down a different, difficult road for a while into a new landscape. It is a landscape of lattices, squares, circles, hexagons, symmetry, and hemispheres. Along the way, we will learn how the internal visual image is constructed and how I see it, how I scan the image and scan light, and how the complete two-dimensional image gives me a three-dimensional perspective. This information may sound new, arcane, or even impossible, but it is all part of explaining what we can know about religious experiences of light.

Ten years after starting to have lucid dreams and soon after my last fullness of light (the near-death experience), in 1985, I began to see lattice imagery occasionally when I woke up, before opening my eyes. Lattice imagery was not dreamed, nor was it, like a mandala, a numinous experience. Nevertheless, the lattices eventually helped me to understand a bit more of what had happened to me when I saw intense light fill the visual field and I floated up. In the concluding chapter of a book on the place of light in mystical experience, the editor, Matthew T. Kapstein, says, "In contrast to the common emphasis on the nonsensorial and even ineffable character of certain religious experiences, experiences of light—except where 'light' is used in a purely metaphorical fashion—belong in the first instance to the phenomenology of vision" (2004b, p. 268). I find this observation to be correct, and I found that my study of lattice imagery led to an understanding of more than just religious experiences of light, but also to how I see in dreams and how I see when awake.

In May, 1985, after I returned from a stay in India related to my doctoral dissertation in Sanskrit, I moved with my family into an apartment building behind the Moorestown Post Office parking lot. Within days, I began to see varieties of scannable two-dimensional lattice patterns when I woke up, before I opened my eyes. What made this possible was that, behind the head of our bed in our new home, large curtain-less casement windows that faced east let the morning sunlight into the room. The bright sunlight reflected off the white walls and ceiling of the room and passed through my eyelids into my eyes. Then, however it is to be explained, I was able to see the lattice patterns. Light, of course, did not shine onto the patterns in my head, because the patterns were internal and the light waves stopped at my retinas. It appeared that the coming of the light somehow energized the image-making properties of my visual field, so that the patterns appeared. Lattice imagery continued to appear on the brighter mornings of spring and summer in 1985 and 1986 and a few more times until 1990. My descriptions of the lattices are based on at least 88 clear observations.

There was always darkness briefly after seeing a dream and before seeing the lattice. In fact, I did not usually see any lattice until I chose to look to see whether it was there. I would first wonder whether there would be a lattice there to see. As I prepared to look, I felt a vague movement in my eyes and then, keeping my eyes shut, I looked at what would normally be the darkness in front of me and I saw the pattern. It was only years later that I understood what that movement in my eyes was, and it will be more fitting for me to explain it later.

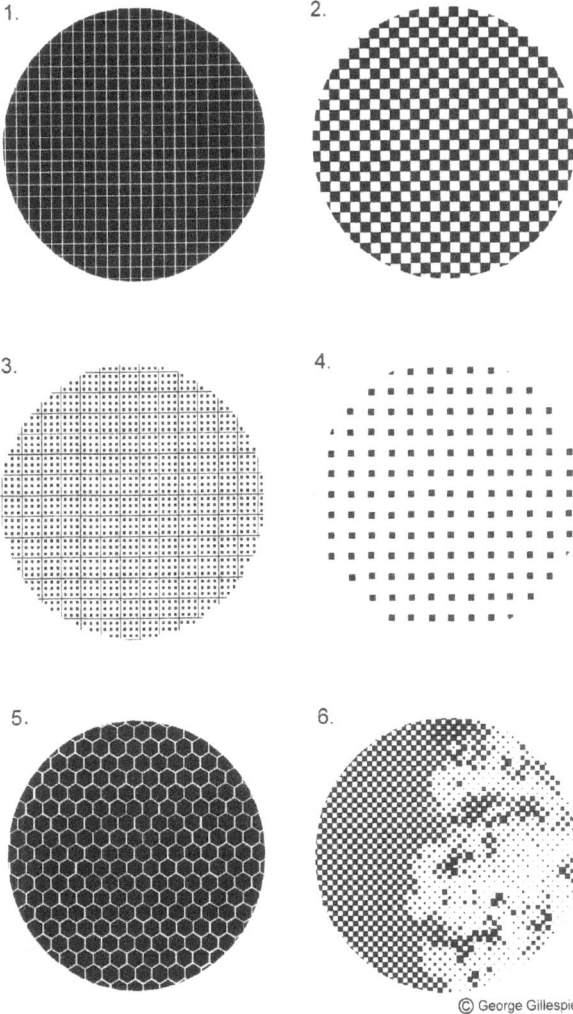

© George Gillespie

Figure 1. Lattice Patterns. 1. Crisscross pattern with lines consisting of light. 2. Chessboard pattern. 3. Crisscross pattern with
dark lines. 4. Crisscross pattern with crossing columns instead of
crossing lines. 5. Vertical-sided hexagon pattern filling the visual
surface. 6. A one-time appearance of a chessboard pattern
across the visual surface, with regular rows of black and white
blocks, but no regularity of block size.

Whenever I saw a lattice, I was newly awake and aware that my body was lying in bed, usually on my back. Because my eyes were shut, I knew that the image was inside me and not showing me something that lay in front of my eyes. The lattice pattern most often filled my visual field, meaning that everywhere I see the perceptual image while I am awake, there I saw the pattern, with no break in its spatial continuity. Just as, by moving my eyes, I scan the perceptual scene while I am awake, I can scan the pattern that I see when I wake up by moving my eyes. Patterns 1.1 through 1.4 can each represent the visual field. As I move my eyes across the pattern, the part of the pattern that I see within the visual field continually changes.

A pattern usually appeared in black and white, but sometimes it included other colors, for example, fuchsia, dark yellow, or maroon. The colors often had an intensity and clarity that can be compared to seeing neon lights. These colors could be called psychedelic.

The most common pattern has been variations of the chessboard design, with alternate squares of black and white, as shown in Figure 1.2. When I mention black and white, I normally do not mean the darkest black or the purest white, for such are rare. The contrast is usually, but not always, between a very dark gray or the darkness I see when I close my eyes and a very pale gray, close to white. Often, all the dark squares of a chessboard pattern contained intricate four-way symmetrical patterns in black and white. Rarely, the lighter squares were other than white, such as lavender, or filled with specks looking like grains of sand. The specks may glitter or not glitter. Sometimes there was such an agitation within the "white" squares that the individual grains could not be discerned from one another. Rarely, the black squares had a smooth, dark lacquered look. Most often, all the squares of the chessboard were the same size during one experience, but sometimes the darker squares were smaller than the lighter squares, meaning that the corners of the lighter squares blended into each other.

The crisscrossing of horizontal and vertical lines or columns has been the second most common form for my lattices. Examples are in Figures 1.1, 1.3, and 1.4. When lines crossed, they consisted of pale light (that is, white) against a dark background, as in 1.1, or were dark lines against a background of white, gray, or another color. Or the pattern included more than just crossing lines, as in Figure 1.3. Figure 1.4 shows the crossing of columns. At rare times, the crossing lines were accompanied by wavy lines of intense neon-type light that formed regular wave lengths and crossed each other at regular intervals in harmony with the rest of the pattern. Each wavy line could lie against a thin straight line, somewhat like a vine clinging to a pole.

The third and much less common pattern has been a lattice of either horizontal-topped or vertical-sided contiguous, uniform hexagons, formed by lines of light as in Figure 1.5. The background to the lines was normally darkness, although once it was lavender. The hexagon patterns did not seem to vary from one occasion to another, except that they were either horizontal-topped or vertical-sided. Only the lines of the hexagons appeared as light.

I have introduced the most common forms. However, unlike with the hexagon lattices, there was enough variety in the chessboard and crisscross patterns that I may never have seen exactly the same pattern twice. Figure 1.6 was a one-time appearance, which I can only approximate in my illustration. The right side of the figure is not quite as chaotic as it may at first appear. In spite of the variation in the relative sizes of the squares, there remains the basic and regular chessboard pattern upon which the variety is laid. Rarely, I saw a lattice formed of horizontal rows of perfect circles.

Imagery that is seen upon waking up is called hypnopompic imagery. If it is seen while falling asleep it is called hypnagogic imagery. If it is seen after ingesting drugs, for example after ingesting "buttons" from the peyote cactus, it is a drug-induced hallucination. Such a hallucination, especially when seen in a religious context, may be thought of as a vision. Oliver Sacks (2012), Siegel & Jarvik (1975), and Ernest Hartmann (1975) refer to imagery that is seen upon waking up as "hypnopompic hallucinations."

Roger N. Shepard (1978) discusses and illustrates his own observations of lattice imagery. Because he illustrates his own patterns, I see that his are of a similar nature to what I have seen. He gives enough details of his lattice appearances that I am confident that my own observations are not unique to myself. Siegel and Jarvik (1975) also mention and illustrate crisscross, chessboard, and hexagon lattices like mine as some of a limited number of elementary hallucinatory form-constants that are brought about through the ingestion of drugs. Elementary form-constants are geometric forms and related imagery (such as dots, blobs, and areas of light) that appear over and over again within drug-induced hallucinations. I was blessed with these spontaneous experiences without the use of drugs.

There are important differences between seeing perceptually and seeing lattice imagery, of course. I see perceptually with my eyes open. On the other hand, light coming through my closed eyelids helps to make my lattice imagery appear, and my eyes themselves do not observe the lattices. Seeing lattices is one kind of eyeless seeing. True, I do move my eyes to scan the image, but my eyes do not see the image.

Although seeing externally using the eyes and seeing internally without the eyes happen differently, directing my attention to (or looking at) what I choose to see happens the same way for perception and lattice imagery. When I direct my attention to the window of the house across the street, the window is the only thing that I am directly looking at or toward. The rest of the visual field I see, but I do not look at it, nor do I see it as well. It is true that I see what I look directly at in most detail because that part of the visual field corresponds to the fovea in the center of the retina, which picks up more of the detail during perception.

However, the fovea, being part of the eye, does not play a part when I direct my attention internally to the hypnopompic image. With lattice imagery, the focus of my attention also, automatically, lies in the center of what I see, and I am therefore able to see that part best. The rest of the lattice-filled visual field I do not see so well, because I do not look at the rest directly, just as happens during visual perception. In both cases, with perception and hypnopompic imagery, it is a strain to take notice of the rest of the visual field beyond the central area of attention. When I scan the image, the focus of my attention remains in the center of the visual field. Later, I will treat attention with more detail.

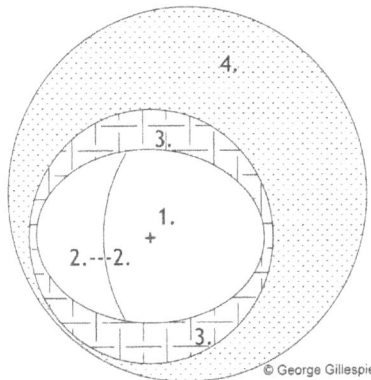

Figure 2. Relative shapes and sizes of visual fields and the visual surface: 1) Monocular perceptual visual field; 2) Binocular perceptual visual field; 3) Elementary visual field; 4) Visual surface. The plus sign marks the center of the elementary visual field and the focal point of all directed visual attention. The elementary visual field (No. 3) is portrayed as located in the lower left of the visual surface as though the eye has stopped there in the midst of scanning the visual surface.

26. The Circle Within a Circle

The visual field of the lattice pattern is not the same size or shape as the perceptual visual field. If I close one eye while I am awake and then open the other eye also, I see that my binocular visual field is larger, that is, wider, than my monocular visual field. When I see the world with both eyes, the visual field of what I see is roughly oval. It is wider than it is high. It is easiest to see the center part where my attention is focused, and I may not notice the outer reaches of the visual field at all.

Figure 2, number 1 indicates roughly the shape and relative size of the monocular visual field, the area seen when only one eye is open during visual perception. Figure 2, number 2 represents the binocular perceptual visual field, that is, the area I see when I perceive with both eyes open. When I see a lattice filling its visual field, as most lattices do, I see that its visual field (Figure 2, number 3, which includes areas 1 and 2) extends higher and lower than the perceptual visual field and reaches just slightly farther back to the sides. In fact, I can see clearly that the visual field for lattices is round, when I think to check on it, because, unlike the perceptual image, the whole lattice visual field is, as a rule, equally precise, clear, and bright. The pattern illustrations in Figure 1.1 through 1.4 are round because the visual field filled with a geometric pattern is round. I will deal with the size and shape of Figures 1.5 and 1.6 soon.

I call the larger visual field of lattice imagery the elementary visual field, because elementary imagery (geometric and related imagery), in contrast to perceptual or percept-like (dream) imagery, may appear anywhere within the round visual field, including beyond the perceptual visual field. The center of the elementary visual field, where directed attention is always located (when there is directed attention), is shown in the figure by the plus sign.

The elementary visual field is not limited in size or shape by the structure of the head around the eyes, as the perceptual image is, because lattice imagery is not created through perceptual processes. Nor is it dream imagery or like dream imagery, which normally simulates perceptual seeing and therefore has a more percept-like visual field. On some of the darker mornings, the lattice pattern fills only the perceptual visual field. It is as though light reaching the retina, largely coming through my eyelids, provides a certain boost of energy that usually helps the whole elementary visual field of image to show itself, but sometimes the light is only intense enough to produce imagery within the limits of the perceptual visual field.

A lattice pattern not only usually fills the elementary visual field, but as I move my eyes, that is, as I scan the pattern, I see that the lattice itself reaches in every direction as far as I can turn my eyes. My scanning eyes do not look at or see the pattern, meaning they do not pick up light waves coming from the pattern, but for every position of my scanning eyes, my visual field reveals a particular section of the total scannable pattern. Turning my head does not change or affect what I see.

I call the whole scannable area the visual surface, which in Figure 2 is indicated by number 4. Number 4 includes all the area within the outer circumference of the diagram. To get an idea of the size of the visual surface, you can close your eyes and move your eyes around in as large an area as you can. That scanning covers the visual surface. I compare the sizes and shapes of the visual fields and visual surface in Figure 2. The figure cannot be drawn precisely, in part because there is no way for me to measure these areas and there most likely are individual differences.

I can move my eyes to scan and study the pattern, because the pattern itself remains unmoving and unchanging for three to ten minutes before it fades away. Because the limits of my eye movement determine the limits of the total pattern over the visual surface, the pattern's total reach (the circumference of area 4) is considerably larger than the elementary visual field (the circumference of area 3). When I scan a lattice, I move area 3 within area 4. When my eyes are at rest, the center of my elementary visual field appears to rest naturally in the center of the visual surface, and thus in the center of the extended pattern.

The scannable lattice image tends to be of equal clarity throughout the visual surface. However, I see the center of any lattice visual field, located at the plus sign, more easily than the rest of the visual field, not because my attention to the center makes the image clearer, brighter, or more detailed (it doesn't), but because it is always difficult to look beyond the center of the visual field where my attention is located, just as it is difficult to do so during visual perception. I can do no more than try to take notice of what lies beyond the focus of my attention. How much one easily sees or notices beyond the focal point during visual imagery or visual perception varies with people.

When I move the visual field around the visual surface, that is, when I scan the extended image, I see that the visual surface itself is round. The limits of my eye movement not only demonstrate the limits of the lattice pattern that I scan, but also shows the outer limits of all appearances of visual imagery of any kind. When I scan and count the rows of the pattern from top to bottom of the visual surface and from left to right, I see that the number of rows is the same, both left to right and top to bottom.

Naturally, as I scan, because the focus of my attention remains in the center of the elementary visual field, I can never direct my attention to the border of either the perceptual or elementary visual field, but, if the brightness of the image on the border is intense, I will notice the border. Figure 2 shows the round elementary visual field (number 3) in the lower left of the round visual surface (number 4), as though I have stopped moving my eyes at that point during my scanning.

By scanning, I see that, within the visual surface, chessboard and crisscross patterns have varied from 10 rows by 10 across the middle (ten rows up and down and ten left to right, crossing in the center of the visual surface) to somewhere around 100 by 100 rows (which I can only estimate). Hexagons, however, have always appeared to be roughly 20 rows by 20. In other words, my individual chessboard and crisscross squares vary in size from observation to observation, but my visual field of hexagons does not vary in size, or at least has not done so. This means also that in Figure 1, because the size of the squares of the pattern may vary, patterns 1 through 4 may illustrate the pattern filling the elementary visual field or filling the visual surface. The pattern of hexagons represents only how it fills the visual surface. Pattern number 6 represents the image at one time over the complete visual surface.

If my eyes are open when I see the lattice, the center of my attention for both lattice imagery and my bedroom always lies in the center of the elementary visual field, shown by the plus sign in Figure 2. The perceptual and the elementary visual fields have the same location of their focus of attention, as does also the monocular visual field. Whether I scan the external world or scan a visual image that exists only internally, I move my visual field within the limits of the visual surface (area 4) and any directed attention remains in that common center.

The much larger size of the elementary visual field in comparison with the perceptual visual field explains why geometric or certain light imagery may be reported by some people as appearing beyond the boundaries of the perceptual visual field. For example, when I told of my experience of light in section 13, the light appeared above what I felt to be my head and far above the perceptual visual field.

Strictly speaking, only the part of the total pattern that lies within my visual field at any moment is a visual image, because that is all that I see at any time. Whatever part of the total pattern that I am not seeing, but which will appear again as I scan the image, I think of as potential image. It is, in some manner, out of view ready to be seen again.

When it is time to analyze the fullness of light, we will see that the intense light also fills the elementary visual field and thus extends beyond the borders of the perceptual visual field. It fills as well the visual surface as I move my eyes. This analysis will also help in the later discussion of dream imagery and of what I call stable intense lights, of which the fullness of light is the most intense form of light. The point that should be noted here is that although the fullness of light is a unique religious event for me, its phenomenology is not isolated from other types of visual events.

27. The Lattice Hemisphere

While studying lattice imagery, I came upon a puzzling paradox. By a close examination of the lattice images, I could see that the lattice image proves to be flat and fills the visual field with strictly parallel lines and precise squares, just like the lattices look that are illustrated in Figure 1. However, at other times, I could also see the lattice visual field as a recessed hemisphere that I look into. But how could I see both at different times?

I'll start with the image as flat. I found that the easiest way to examine the complete image was to scan the whole lattice over the visual surface. Because the focus of my attention as I scanned was naturally always in the center of the visual field, I was studying details only at the center of any visual field as I moved my eye. In that way, I could move most of the image piece by piece into the center of the visual field, and thus examine most of the pattern closely. By "most," I mean that the center of the visual field would itself never touch the border of the visual surface, although I could be aware of the border.

Although I could not examine the smallest details away from the center of the visual field, where my attention was forced to remain, I saw that the center was always flat wherever I looked, with straight lines and precise squares. When I traced the major lines and columns of a chessboard or crisscross lattice closely in order to count the number of rows vertically and horizontally across the visual surface, I only saw the image as flat. The precise continuity and regularity of the image, as demonstrated in Figure 1, numbers 1 through 4, assured me that every image as a whole was actually flat and contained undistorted lattice imagery throughout the scannable visual surface.

The major vertical and horizontal lines or columns shown especially in Figures 1.1, 1.2, 1.3, and 1.4 demonstrate the strict regularity of the image across the visual field and the visual surface. All major vertical lines and columns, anywhere within the visual field and the visual surface as I scan, are always in strict alignment with the vertical axis of my head. Because I have just awakened and my eyes are shut, I am always aware that my head lies around the image, and my head does not restrict the size of the visual field as it does during perception.

The vertical lines always divide my awareness of my head into left and right. All major horizontal lines and columns are perpendicular to the vertical lines and columns and perpendicular to the vertical axis of my head. When I move my head, I make no change in the pattern, but when I move my eyes, the major lines and columns remain strictly either vertical or horizontal as I see them in the center of the moving visual field.

Eventually, I came to realize that when I scanned the pattern, I tended to ignore the imagery that was always lying beyond the center of my focus, although I knew that the whole visual field contained imagery. Part of the problem here is that I have a narrow focus of attention. What I did see proved that the image was strictly flat, but I also had hints that I was scanning a curved surface, in part due to my eye movement, which in perceptual terms kept looking in different directions as I scanned. The fact was that the visual field only faced one direction although my eyes, which didn't really do the seeing, "looked" in different directions.

When I eventually did take notice of the outer areas of the visual field, even though I could not look at them directly, I saw that the pattern across the whole elementary visual field actually curved back towards me on all sides of my central focus and actually formed a perfectly smooth-looking hemispheric dome that I looked into. In fact, the visual field formed a dome that was a distorted version of my flat lattice imagery. I now understand that the creation of a domed lattice from a flat lattice is due to my constant perceptual mindset. When I restrict myself to the center of the image where my attention is directed, I neglect seeing the whole dome of image, which is actually almost always fully there to see. In short, when I study only the center of a lattice image, I see it all as flat. When I see more than the center where my attention is focused, I see that the pattern is concave. There is more to the story, but that comes later.

E1-A1-E1 elementary visual field
A1-A central lline of sight
D-D1 limits of perceptual visual field

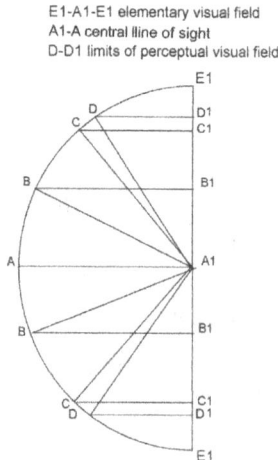

Figure 3. The spatial relationship between the elementary image located on the flat visual field and how I see it with a perceptual mindset. E1-A1-E1 represents a vertical cut through the center of

the flat elementary visual field. E1-A-E1 represents the hemispheric projection of the image that occurs with the perceptual mindset. A1, the center of the base of the hemispheric projection, is my viewpoint from which I look to the left. A is the image of A1 when I see it as at a distance. A1-A becomes what I think of as my central line of sight. B1 is seen as being at B, C1 as being at C, etc. A1-B, A1-C, and so on represent other lines of sight that I assume I have from the viewpoint (A1). This figure also shows how a light located at the top of the visual field, that is, at the upper E1, appears as if it is located straight above the head or the eye, which seems to be at A1.

In Figure 3, E1-A1-E1 represents a vertical cut through the center of the flat elementary visual field, with the upper E1 representing the top of the visual field and the lower E1, the bottom of the visual field. I am facing left in the figure.

When I decide to check the darkness to see whether there is a pattern there, my attention is automatically directed to the center of the visual field at A1, and I am aware that I see a lattice pattern. Because I am used to seeing perceptually, meaning that I have an automatic perceptual mindset, I see the center of the pattern (A1) as though it is at a distance from me at A. In fact, with the perceptual mindset, I project the whole flat round image (E1-A1-E1) into a world that I see around me (E1-A-E1).

I may at first only direct my attention to the center, at A, which is presented to me as flat, because I am not directing my attention toward the curved part. While keeping my attention on A, but taking notice of more of the visual field, I become aware that the pattern that I see curves back on all sides, making a smooth hemisphere (E1-A-E1) that I look into. The apex of the hemisphere remains at A, even as I scan, and my viewpoint remains at A1, which lies at the center of the base of the hemisphere. In perception, I would see only D1-A1-D1 as D-A-D. However, seeing the lattice with a perceptual mindset, I can, when I try, see the lattice as E1-A-E1. If I noticed only part of the lattice, I would see that part as part of the hemisphere.

The flat unprojected lattice (along E1-A1-E1) is without distortion. When that lattice is seen as a hemisphere, the part of the created dome farthest from the center (D1-E1) has the greatest distortion. For example, between E1 and D1 it has the least visual image in proportion to its projected enlargement (E1-D). At the very center of the visual field, where my attention is directed, I see the pattern with minor or no distortion, and so it looks flat. This is helped by the fact that the image actually is flat.

My attention does not work as it does for most people. My attention is not visually broad. Therefore I am, I hope, leaving out of this explanation any further reference to my personal differences, where I can. A discussion of my narrow focus of attention appears in Gillespie (2017). I believe that what I say further about attention, however, is still relevant.

The continuity and uniformity of the domed lattice, in spite of its distorted squares and curved lines, creates the look of a smooth surface on the inside of the dome, with all parts of the dome seeming to lie equally distant from my viewpoint. Even when the visual field is not full of image, as much lattice as I do see looks like it is part of a receding hemisphere. Mardi Horowitz mentions that for hallucinators seeing drug-induced imagery, "the sense of a receding center to the visual field … is a definite recurrent formal element" (1975, p. 178).

When I scan the lattice, say by moving my eyes from left to right, I can see that the pattern to the right of center looks less and less distorted as I move that part of the image into the center of the visual field. When that part is in the center, meaning that I am looking directly at that center, the image looks correct, regular, and flat. As I continue to move my eyes to the right, that center part of the pattern now moves away to the left and begins to look distorted again, and moreso until it moves off the other side of the visual field.

28. The Disappearance
of the Hemisphere

The dome of the distorted lattice image appears automatically when I take notice beyond the center of the visual field, because my perceptual mindset is automatic. I found that even when I do not look directly at any part of the image, I see the image that seems to surround me, just as the world surrounds me when I am awake. However, with lattice imagery, I also found that I could choose not to see with the perceptual mindset. When I decided to look at the lattice visual field as a whole, without directing my attention to any particular location, the dome or hemisphere disappeared. I saw the whole image, the whole visual field, as flat. When I directed my attention to the image, the dome was created. Directing my attention forced the image to become the dome.

When I forgot eyes, visual perception, three-dimensionality, distances, light waves, retinas, reflecting surfaces, the focusing of attention, and viewpoint, I found that I saw the lattice flat and undistorted, which it proved to be when I scanned the image. By not directing my attention to the image, which also means by not looking at some location on the image, I do not create a viewpoint from which I look or a focal point that I look towards. I eliminate my perceptual mindset. However, it does seem that I have to purposefully eliminate the mindset, because if I just don't think about it, I retain the perceptual mindset.

Eventually, I found that I could freely take turns, first seeing the image automatically with a perceptual mindset, that is, with no effort, as a receding hemisphere of distorted lattice imagery and then, by resisting my tendency to look directly at the image and by seeing the visual field of the lattice as a whole, looking at no specific location, I see the flat surface of the undistorted lattice. When I see the lattice without thinking perceptually, I cannot discern any of the pattern's finest details, but I see the whole pattern with equal clarity across the visual

field, even when the image is not bright. All it takes for me to
see it first one way and then the other is to intentionally look at
one part of the pattern and create the apex of the dome there,
and then intentionally consider it as a whole, without directing
my attention anywhere. I could rapidly take turns seeing the
image as flat and as a dome, at will.

Seeing the lattice visual field without hemisphere, viewpoint, or point of focus results not only in seeing the flatness of
the image, but in finding that every part of the image, every
square has the look of being seen face on—face on at every
point. There is no distortion anywhere. When I see the image as
flat, I imagine no radiating lines of sight as if from an eye. Nor
are there any angles of vision. Because directing my attention to
a location within the lattice image has such a different result
from seeing the visual field as a whole, I believe that it is
misleading to speak of directing my attention to the whole.
Seeing the visual field as a whole is to not direct attention.

Earlier I mentioned that when I woke up and wanted to see
whether there was a lattice there to see, I felt a movement in my
eyes as I prepared to look. I now understand that the movement in my eyes was due to my transition to the perceptual
mindset. I was getting ready to direct my attention.

I use the chessboard and crisscross lattices to talk about the
flat visual field, the perceptual mindset, and the lattice hemisphere that is created, because I believe that is the easiest way
to visualize what I am saying. However, seeing the lattice of
contiguous hexagons happens in the same way. The hexagons
appear to be without distortion when I see the pattern as a
whole, without directing my attention to it, whether it is a field
of vertical-sided or of horizontal-topped hexagons. When I
attend to the pattern with a perceptual mindset, the hexagons
are projected into a receding hemisphere. As with lattice
imagery, there is greater distortion of the hexagons as they are
distanced from the center of the visual field. In all ways, the
seeing of hexagons parallels the seeing of the chessboard and

crisscross patterns, and, in the same way, the vertical or horizontal lines of the hexagons, when the whole is seen as a flat visual field, are in strict vertical and horizontal alignment with my body image, particularly my head. With lattices or with any elementary imagery, the hemisphere and viewpoint that I automatically create is my unending attempt to understand what I see in terms of a three-dimensional world around me. The hemispheric projection of the image will explain also how I understand perceptual and dream imagery, as well as experiences of the fullness of light and any other seeing of color and visual form. Lattices and other elementary imagery are understood "correctly" only when seen without a perceptual mindset.

29. Seer, Seeing, and Seen

Conceiving how one can see an internal visual image, literally of color and visual form, whether dream, hallucinatory, or perceptual, has been such a problem for philosophers and other theorists that many of them have even concluded that there can be no such thing as an internal visual image (for example, Dennett, 1991, 1992; Gibson, 1986; C. McGinn, 2004). It is usually stated that there can be no visual image, because there can be no little person in the head (a homunculus) or an internal eye, which would be needed to look at the image.

Daniel Dennett (1991, 1992), one of the most extreme in denying the possibility of the subjective experience of visual imagery, stresses that there can be no "pictures in the head," no "Cartesian Theater" in the head that would require an audience. "[P]ictures in the head will require eyes in the head to appreciate them (to say nothing of good lighting)" (1991, p. 52). Since there can be no visual image of any kind, he says, there are no such things as visual phenomena or colors. There only seem to be colors. Colors are only "complex dispositional states of the brain" (*ibid.*, p. 431). However, I will tell what I found through analyzing the colors and forms of my lattice imagery.

Although I will primarily talk about how I see the lattice imagery that comes to me spontaneously, the questions of how I see the image apply to all seeing of visual imagery, and in fact the varieties of darkness also, all that appears within the visual field. How do I see the perceptual image, the dream image, hallucinations, or the fullness of light? When I move my eyes to scan the visual surface, my eyes never do the seeing. In dreams also, my eyes may scan, but they never see what is going on in the dream. The image appears without the help of my eyes. This means that I do not have or need dream eyes (more on that later).

The visual image is never in front of my eyes. It is within me. I see the image whether my eyes are open or closed. Seeing any visual image is a form of eyeless seeing. Through my eyes and their retinas, I may create an internal perceptual image. But the question remains: How do I see the lattice image, or any visual image?

As I described in the last section, I found that when I stop looking at a particular location on the lattice and see the lattice visual field as a whole without a perceptual mindset, and also when I examine all of a lattice piece by piece, I see that the lattice, as also its visual field, is actually flat. I found also that every piece of the flat lattice has the look of being presented face-on and undistorted. Every line is straight. Every square is seen to be precisely square. The whole presentation has the look of graph paper. This is the manner in which I see it when the visual field is not distorted by seeing with a perceptual mindset.

The lattice pattern, and thus also its visual field, looks as though I were seeing it by means of a mass of parallel lines of sight all perpendicular to the flat visual field. However, I do not and cannot see the visual field by means of either one or many lines of sight. In fact, any suggestion of lines of sight would necessitate some kind of eyes or eye substitutes somewhere and would create a version of the homunculus problem. A mass of lines of sight would require a mass of homunculi, each looking along its own line of sight. There are no lines of sight.

The precise, undistorted lattice pattern, as it appears without the perceptual mindset, suggests that I actually see it face-on at every "point" of the pattern, even though I am not normally aware that I see it that way. That means that, with any kind of visual image, I see the image and the visual field face-on with no distance or separation from the image all across the visual field. The lattice image looks like it is constructed to be seen that way, and that is how I see it without the perceptual mindset. But there is no visual evidence of an "I" (me) of any sort facing the image. Seeing may need no more than for the image to appear through unknown processes, and I say, "I see." My seeing is spread across the whole visual field, face-on, even as I scan. The concept we are left with is that the image itself is not only my seeing, it is the part of me that sees. There is no separation of seer and seen. Every part of the visual field is a nonduality of seer and seen.

Let's look again at Figure 3 to show how my seeing the visual image face-on at every point works. The visual field in Figure 3 is represented by a vertical cut (E1-A1-E1) through the center of the visual field (A1). I see the image face-on at every point of E1-A1-E1, with my facing to the left. With my perceptual mindset, I see every part of the image as together creating a recessed hemisphere (E1-A-E1) that I look into. I project every part forward. I see the image at A1 as if it is located at A, where it is the object of my attention. A1 remains my viewpoint and A1-A plays the role of my central line of sight. Because I see every point face-on, I see B1 at B, C1 at C, etc. but I believe that my lines of sight are A1-B, A1-C, etc. Any image lying between D1 and E1, as when I see a lattice, I understand to be located between D and E1 and that part of the created hemisphere appears to lie outside the perceptual visual field. What I see at either E1 appears to be located on the periphery of the visual field, but since my attention is automatically directed forward to the center, I may not notice unless the image there is very bright.

30. Visual Perception

I wrote my earliest analysis of visual perception years ago in some detail (Gillespie, 1990), but now for the sake of completeness and for bringing my writing up-to-date with my present thinking, I will give the basic details here. This is what logically follows from what I learned from studying lattice imagery.

I will discuss the perceptual image using Figure 3 again. Only this time, let the figure represent first how I perceive externally whatever is located around me. The whole figure then represents the view from above my location at A1 and the location of whatever I see along D-A-D. While standing or moving, I am looking from A1 directly at a tree, a child, or whatever is located at A. My central line of sight is A1-A. I see also, but do not look directly at, everything else within my perceptual limits (D-A-D). While I direct my attention to A, A1-B is my line of sight to B, and A1-C is my line of sight to C, etc. The Ds represent the limits of what I see but, with my attention directed to A, it is difficult for me to notice the limits of the visual field to the sides, above, and below. I can only guess the exact limits of the perceptual visual field, which, in any case, may vary in size or shape among individuals.

Next let Figure 3 represent a horizontal cross section of my flat perceptual image (D1-A1-D1) cut through my focus point at A1. The limited perceptual dome that I project forward with my perceptual mindset is D-A-D. It is possible for me to project forward the dome only because I see the image face-on at every point. To "project forward" simply means to see the image in terms of the three-dimensional world around me. What I saw externally at A appears on the flat visual field at A1 and I see it internally as if at A. What I saw externally at B, I see internally at B1 and I project it forward internally to see it at B. The same with C1 and D1 on both sides of my viewpoint at A1. I have created a what-it-looks-like of color and visual forms out of a world that has no look, no color, and no visual form until I create it internally.

Internally, while A1-A represents the central line of sight that I create, other lines of sight from my viewpoint seem to reach out from A1 to B, C, and D. Those apparent lines of sight reflect the original lines of sight from my eyes to what I saw. However, no lines of sight from my viewpoint at A1 to my projected image actually exist. Therefore, the image on the flat visual field must be distributed so that every part of it will correctly portray my view when projected strictly forward. In a manner of speaking, the unprojected image is a flattened-down version of the scene that I perceive and of the dome that I create out of the image.

Whereas with lattice imagery the continuity and uniformity of the lattice pattern always results in the look of a smooth inner surface of the dome that I see, with visual perception the world has no look of a smooth surface. The perceptual dome will show little continuity of lines, little uniformity of pattern, and no equality of distance from the viewpoint. The world is not constructed like that. Although the directions of seeing from the viewpoint are indicated precisely by their location within the visual field (for example, what I see in the direction of A1-B is seen at B1, which I see as if at B), distances are not precisely seen. For that we rely on stereopsis and cues to distance.

In binocular vision, I experience the alignment of my two retinal images to make a single fused image (De Valois & De Valois, 1988; Hubel, 1988; Julesz, 1971). The alignment results in stereopsis in the center of the visual field, which is largely credited for our seeing three-dimensionally. However, three-dimensional seeing does not solely depend on the creation of a narrow area of stereopsis around the center of the image. The whole projected dome of the visual field created by my perceptual mindset contributes to my seeing the world three-dimensionally, even with vision that relies on only one eye. So far, analyzing lattice imagery has given me no insight into stereopsis.

IV

Dream

---

31. Dreams and Imagination

Colin McGinn claims that "if dreams consist of images, then we would predict that no concurrent images, could be formed, since the imaginative faculty is already being used. ... I can have only the dream experience—with no other contemporaneous exercises of imagination" (2004, p. 78).

McGinn seems to find virtually no distinction between dreaming and imagining. The classification of dream imagery with visual imagination and visual memory, however, must lead to a confusion of categories. Visual imagining and visual remembering can be classed together, for they are experienced in the same way, and it is difficult to think of either happening without being partly the other. However, visual imagination and memory must be contrasted with hypnopompic, dream, and perceptual imagery, which are experiences of color and visual form, and are, therefore, literally experiences of seeing.

A series of experiments during lucid dreaming helped me to experience the difference between visual dream imagery and visual memory or imagination. When awake, I can look about me while voluntarily recalling or imagining, correctly or incorrectly, what another place looks like. I found that in a lucid dream I could do the same. I could remain aware of what was occurring visually, while remembering or imagining something else. Although activity within the dream visual field tends to lessen when I try to remember or imagine something, visual imagery remains just as full and vivid as ever.

In a series of lucid dreams, while retaining a visual scene by keeping my (dreamed) eyes open, I was able to recall with varying degrees of detail what my grandmother's house looked like. I did this once while looking at a horizon of trees, in another dream while running along a mountain road, once more while walking down some stairs, and once again while I was fingering a plastic tablecloth that had magenta-colored dots. Although my visual memory was never as complete as it is while I am awake, I experienced the memory as I do when awake, without any elimination or disturbance of what I was seeing. My memory of my grandmother's house was never completely correct in detail, but it was basically her house that I pictured in my mind.

Alan Worsley (1988) also reports that during lucid dreaming he could imagine things while he experienced the visual imagery of the dream. The content of his imagination would often appear later as part of his visual dream imagery. Mine largely did not.

With some help from Block (1983), Haber (1969, 1979), James (1918), and Nagel (1980), I will suggest some essential differences between visual imagination or memory and literal experiences of color and visual form. When I try to visually imagine or remember, I try to see what is not already within my visual field to see, neither as perceived object nor as image. I can try to imagine or remember whatever I want to. Unlike the perceptual, dream, or hypnopompic image, which I must accept as is, the experience of imagination or memory is intended and under my control.

Ordinarily, what I imagine or remember is imprecise in form and not composed of color in any literal sense. It has no content beyond what I think of, and I can learn nothing new from it. The location of its whole or its parts is indefinite in terms of the visual field, and I cannot scan it by moving my eyes. In fact, there is always something different altogether within the visual field when I try to imagine or remember—for example, perceptual or dream imagery, or even darkness.

Color imagery, on the other hand, such as hypnopompic, dream, or perceptual imagery, is literally seen and is composed of color. As image, it is spatially present, and has a certain objective reality for me, whether as something perceived or as something internal. I have no choice in the matter of details. It is precise in content, color, and form, whether or not it is a clear image and whether I notice all the details or not. At any moment, all parts of color imagery have a specific location within the visual field and visual surface. I may discover, learn, or find something unanticipated through scanning, scrutiny, redirecting my attention, or by chance. Seeing, scanning, scrutiny, precision of detail, and spatiality all mean one thing for visual dreaming and something else for imagining and remembering.

I believe that some people, when they imagine or remember, are able to produce a visual image that they can actually see. I also believe that for some people dream imagery appears to be next to nothing. So we all tend to think of imagery according to our own experience. And I do the same.

32. Dream World

Whenever I experienced the fullness of light, I was asleep. The editors of *The Functions of Dreaming* (Moffitt, Kramer & Hoffmann, 1993) write, "By *dreaming* we refer to any image, thought or feeling attributed by the dreamer to a preawakening state" (p. 2). By this definition, my experiences of the fullness of light would be dreams. Dreaming, in fact, has preceded each experience of the fullness of light, and some dreamed body imagery also commonly has continued into the experience. I also have experienced the fullness of light in continuity from my seeing in the preceding dream. In fact, for a long time, I considered the experiences of the fullness of light to be part of my dreaming.

Eventually I accepted on faith that the experiences were truly what they seemed to be—experiences of the presence of God. Even later than that, I discovered that the light of the fullness that I was seeing was not dream imagery, but belonged to a separate category of imagery that I call stable intense lights. These lights cannot be called dream imagery for reasons that I will explain later. Considering that dreaming is normally the context in which these religious experiences emerge, it is necessary to consider the nature of the dream world, the dream body, and dream seeing.

Seeing in a dream is a simulation of perceiving the world while awake—as though I see one small part of a world as it looks from the viewpoint of my eye or eyes. Therefore, I see the image of my dream world in the way that I perceive the world when I am awake. In Figure 3, the dream image of the world that I see must lie within the flat visual field within the bounds of D1-A1-D1, with my point of attention, as usual, at A1, in the center of the visual field. With my perceptual mindset, I project the image along A1-A, B1-B, and so on, perhaps not always filling the perceptual visual field. Other imagery, of body experience, hearing, and so on, completes the simulation.

How I understand darkness, light, and other colors and the spatial properties and locations of what I see in the dream carries over from how I understand what I see when awake with my eyes open. However, in my dream I tolerate more oddity in what I see. My perceptual mindset helps me to see the flat image correctly. "Correctly" means that I see the flat dream imagery three-dimensionally, which is how I see and understand it when I am awake. Although darkness or brightness in a dream may add to the simulation of my waking experience, darkness is only the lessening or disappearance of the visual image and brightness is only the intensification of the colors of the image.

Although I do not analyze my dream world very deeply while dreaming, I see no evidence that the dream world that I see and feel exists at all beyond my experience of the moment. When I am awake, there is more to see to my left and right, and I may look to the left or right to see it. When I dream, there is nothing to see to my left and right until I turn my head or body and more images appear. What I see while awake is a visual version of what lies before the eyes of my physical body as I move around. Likewise, while dreaming, I assume that the world is being shown to me and that there is more of it where I am not looking, even behind me.

To be precise, the dream world, so called, does not simulate the waking world. It is dream seeing, hearing, and touching that simulates my waking seeing, hearing, and touching the world. Visual dream imagery normally reveals no more of a world than what I see, hear, and feel, for it is created through unconscious processes at work and not through the work of eyes. The visual image of the moment suffices for giving me a world to see. My dream world is not a planet Earth substitute, but a substitute for visual and other modes of perception. There is no world-like way that I got to this place in the dream and there is no other place near it until I experience it. When I close my dreamed eyes, that image of a world disappears and tends not to appear again as it had been, no matter what visual activity follows.

Just as the visual image itself is the whole of the world that I see in a dream, the feeling of standing on the ground or of being touched or supported in a dream is the world that I feel under me and next to me. The world that I touch is only the touch that I feel while I feel it. When I feel that I float up from the ground, floor, or bed, there is no longer any ground, floor, or bed in the dream because the feeling is gone. Dreamed sound is the world as I hear it around me.

A world is created for me, consisting only of the imagery, thoughts, and subjective feelings of the moment. The belief that

I am inside what I see carries over from waking perception to the dream by means of the perceptual mindset and the creation of the receding hemisphere, with its viewpoint and its focus at the apex. The perceptual mindset locates my specific place as the seer within what I see and thus pinpoints the location of my body with its eyes. The same happens during the fullness of light. The belief that what I see lies around me does not carry over into my seeing lattice imagery when I wake up, because then I am aware that my body is actually lying in bed and that the image is located within my head.

The waking world conforms to the laws of physics, chemistry, and clocks and has a certain consistency and continuity from moment to moment, and day to day. Because the dream world conforms only to the way visual imagery, seeing, and dreams work, it is not limited by the physics, chemistry, and clocks of the waking world. Consistency and continuity of dream imagery and narrative from moment to moment and dream to dream cannot be expected.

Sometimes people mention a dream or other imagery that appears to them to be a vision of Heaven or of spiritual beings or of the dead, or a vision of what can actually be seen elsewhere once they wake up, as in remote viewing or precognition. I am not suggesting that none of this can or cannot be so. I do suggest that the two-dimensional visual field of color and visual form that one sees in a dream, vision, or hallucination only simulates perception and cannot ever itself be the three-dimensional place, object, or event that is portrayed. My suggestion that the dream world proves to be image-only neither supports nor denies that the image may truly at times portray or reveal some specific situation, place, or entity that lies beyond itself. However, it does not customarily do so.

33. Dream Body and Dream Eyes

Some people (including myself) normally feel that they are bodily present in their dreams. When I dreamed that I knelt next to the bed, folded my hands, and closed my eyes to pray, I was aware of having a body—what some people may call a dream body. However, the phrase "dream body" seems simply to be a convenient way of talking about dream experience, and does not refer to a complete, three-dimensional body of any sort. Likewise, dream eyes, so to speak, appear not to be eyes at all.

There are five characteristics of dreaming that give me the impression that I have a body with eyes when I dream.

1. My subjective experience of having a body is a substitute for having a body. The body imagery that I experience, such as the feeling of walking, dancing, or floating, the feeling that wind is blowing my loose clothing, the apparent pull of gravity, or the feeling that someone is pinching my leg, I think of at the time as belonging to my body, but no material or three-dimensional body necessarily goes with the feelings. It is as though I have a solid body with three-dimensionality, weight, form, posture, and boundaries, as I do have when I am awake, but I don't.

When I am awake, my subjective body experience informs me about my physical body, with aches, tickles, and the feelings of gravity and movement. I feel its contact with the world. But when I dream, I lose that connection with my sleeping body. Dreamed subjective body imagery simulates informing me about my body. I can bend my arm or walk across the dream room, it seems. However, my subjective body experience gives no evidence of a three-dimensional solid body to go with my experience.

The feeling of kneeling or falling suffices for having a body that can kneel and fall. The feeling and sound of my singing suffices for having a body that sings. The feeling of eating bread or tasting cinnamon suffices for having a body that dream food nourishes. And because I seem to have a body, I believe that it is, as usual, complete with eyes.

2. As for turning my eyes and seeing a man sitting next to me on the bed, I apparently do actually turn the eyes of my sleeping body when I need to and not some eyes that belong to a dream body. I turn my eyes while dreaming just as I turn my eyes when I scan my lattices. Scanning with my eyes is not a simulation. I can scan my eyes while seeing lattices and my bedroom at the same time. Later, I will also show how I move my body's eyes while dreaming and while scanning certain non-dream lights that I call stable intense lights at the same time. No scanning dream eyes are needed.

3. My visual dream image may portray my arms or hand or the lower part of my body from the viewpoint of my eyes as I look at them or portray my face as if in a mirror. So it appears that I see my body or a reflection of my body, but I am only seeing a visual image of my body. My subjective body experience is normally coordinated with what I see of my body, just as happens in waking life. I also see the images of people seeming to look at me. The visual image of Joe or my family looking at me gives me the impression that they see my body. However, what I see of myself or of others looking at me is only the visual image simulating what I might see during waking perception.

4. Simply because I see when I dream, I believe that I am seeing with eyes, and having eyes seems to mean that I have a body with eyes. However, no dream eyes are needed in order to have a dream image appear. Unconscious processes determine what the image is to be, not my eyes or retinas. Even if I lose awareness of the rest of my body imagery, as sometimes happens in the fullness of light, the fact that I continue to see light makes me feel that I still have eyes to see with, and thus I believe that my body is still, at least partly, there, even when it isn't.

5. Just as when I am awake, the perceptual mindset presents me with a viewpoint, and the apex of the receding dome presents me with an image of what I am looking at or towards. I see everything as facing me from different directions, just as when I am awake. Everything that I see implies that I see from one location where I believe I have eyes. The percept-like image itself places me and my eyes in a precise location within the dream world that I see, except that no eye or retina has produced the image and no eye is needed in order to see the image. I scan what appear to be my surroundings when I dream, but in reality I am only moving my visual field over the visual surface and seeing what the visual field presents.

These experiences suffice for making me believe that I have a body that sees when I dream. No solid or pseudo-solid dream body is needed. That subjective experience may not even supply the experience of a whole body—only as much of a body as is needed for the dream.

> In a dream I was examining closely some kind of instru-ment that I was holding in my hands. My attention was only on what I was holding. Something across the room attracted my attention and I wanted to walk over to the other side of the room to see it closely. However, I could not move away. I couldn't even tell whether I was sitting or standing up. I was not dreaming the lower part of my body. I had nothing to move and I was stuck there.

When in a dream I concentrate on the darkness or light that I see and thereby direct attention away from my body, I lose awareness of my body imagery and it diminishes. The dis-appearance of body imagery is no doubt made easier because no three-dimensional, solid dream body is disappearing. Dreamed body experience disappears and my seeing doesn't disappear with it, because my dreamed seeing has nothing to do with my dreamed body.

34. Dreaming My Bedroom

I have had a number of lucid dreams in which perceptual imagery originating in the bedroom played a part in the dream. These dreams bridge perception and dreaming. I have recorded perceptual imagery as appearing in my dreams twice when I was not lucid, five times when I was lucid, and as a possible explanation in two more lucid dreams. I'll tell about one such dream.

In July of 1977, I was passing through Delhi on my way to Hyderabad in South India to start teaching at a new (for me) seminary. I picked up Carlos Castaneda's *Journey to Ixtlan: The Lessons of Don Juan* (1972), his third book about what he learned from don Juan, a Mexican sorcerer. I began reading it on the plane to Hyderabad. I had earlier read his *A Separate Reality*.

In *Journey to Ixtlan*, don Juan begins to teach Castaneda about *dreaming*. Castaneda uses the italics for the word dreaming to indicate that he is not talking about ordinary dreaming. Some in the lucid dreaming community believe that Castaneda is talking about lucid dreaming, although he does not mention "lucid dreaming."

In 1975, while living in Assam I had spontaneously begun to have lucid dreams, but I had never heard of lucid dreaming. I had had 43 "known dreams" (as I called them) by time I read of don Juan's *dreaming* in Castaneda's book, and it did not dawn on me that he might be talking about the kind of dreams that I had been experiencing.

In the book, Castaneda is told by don Juan that he can train himself to go and see actual places as they really are at the time of dreaming, especially if he takes a nap in the afternoon, when there is daylight. It is easier if he chooses a place of power to go to. Another lesson that don Juan teaches, though not about dreaming, is that by keeping the eyes unfocused and making a double image of an object, one can see between the two images at times indications of the object's nature not seen in ordinary reality. I read Castaneda with a good amount of skepticism.

Don Juan's teachings turned out to be a prelude to my dream during my afternoon nap at the seminary the next day. I was sleeping in the guest room of the acting principal and had managed to finish all of the book except the last chapter before I fell asleep. This was the dream that came to me that afternoon.

> I was standing in a room next to a bright open stairwell that led somewhere down below the floor. There was no railing around the stairwell to prevent people from falling into it. Beyond the stairwell, there was a pair of connected doors. Several times I started toward the doors, but caught myself in time from falling into the stairwell which lay in the way. So I stopped trying to reach the doors.
>
> I commented to someone that I knew I was dreaming. I also "knew" that I was seeing the actual doors of the room where I was sleeping, although I can't say that I really knew where I was. I did not know what was beyond the doors. I felt that I was in some way doing what don Juan suggested that Castaneda should do. I was seeing an actual place as it was while I was dreaming.
>
> I also remembered what don Juan taught about looking at something with unfocused eyes. I unfocused my eyes while looking at the doors. I got a blurred vision of the doors and nothing else.

When I woke up, it was about 5pm. My bedroom was filled with daylight. I had been seeing my bedroom while dreaming, but the details of the room had been transformed for the dream. My standing-up head in the dream had now become my head lying on its side in the bed. The wall that lay beyond my head had been the ceiling in my dream room, with the foot of my bed being the edge of the stairwell that I was standing next to.

The pair of doors in the dream coincided with the pair of doors in my bedroom, for they lay in the same direction from my eyes when I awoke as they had in the dream and filled the same space within the visual field. In the dream, however, the doors were vertical to my eyes, as doors should look when one is standing up. However, upon awakening, the doors became roughly horizontal in relationship to my eyes, because I was lying on my side in the bed. The pair of doors formed a rough square, so that the division between the doors, as I saw them, actually changed first for the dream and then again for waking up. My apparently open eyes could see the transformed dream room clearly, because the daylight was carried over into the dream.

In this example, perceptual imagery or a transformation of perceptual imagery entered into the experience of the dream. Major lines and forms within the perceptual scene from the viewpoint of my eyes in bed were preserved, while the whole of the scene was transformed into the dream image. The lighting of the room was carried over into the dream. My understanding of what I saw in the dream was in accord with the dream transformation of the bedroom, not with the room as it actually was. I had somehow felt that I "recognized" the two doors and knew that they were the doors of my room, although I was actually barely familiar with the room when I was awake.

During the dream, my moving eyes not only scanned my bedroom perceptually from the edge of my bed to the doors on the other side of the room and from door to door, but, by scanning the bedroom, I scanned the dream imagery at the same time, including the stairwell, that was created from the view of the room. The "dream eyes" (so to speak) that I experienced moving when I scanned the room and when I crossed my eyes were the eyes in my sleeping head, for that is the only way I could scan the actual bedroom while scanning the dream. My retinas functioned only in the perception of my bedroom, while I had hallucinated (dreamed) the transformations of the perceived room. I had no memory of moving my body or head. The colors and forms of the dream imagery were integrated with the colors and forms of the percept to make one image.

As for don Juan's suggestion that Castaneda see a real place while dreaming, I did do that, to some extent. Although I saw the room transformed, I did see the major lines of the room as they really appeared perceptually, with the help of the sunlight. However, I didn't choose ahead of time the place I wanted to see. Don Juan suggested that Castaneda choose a place of power to see while dreaming. However, I did see the real guest room of the acting principal of the seminary (a place of power?). Obviously Castaneda did influence my dream, even though the memory of his instructions was incomplete.

Before July was over, after having 48 "known dreams," I found in a Hyderabad book store Ann Faraday's *Dream Power*, in which I could read a short discussion of lucid dreaming. Now I knew there were others having dreams like mine, and they were called "lucid dreams."

35. A Map of Bhutan

Another experience of mine also supports the conclusion that during dreaming my eyes move in a scanning manner, and that this movement is equivalent to the scanning of lattice imagery. My example is of a stilled dream image, which I saw the morning of November 4, 1986.

I awoke and lay quietly on my back in bed without opening my eyes. I remembered that I was looking at a book in my dream and had just turned the page. Although I was distracted by waking up, I realized that I was still seeing a large page of the book up close to me as a bright, clear, and still image. In the image I saw my left hand still holding the book, although the hand did not correspond to the real position of my left hand that I was then aware of.

I remembered from the dream that I was looking at an atlas and seeing a map of Bhutan. Bhutan itself was colored dark green. The areas surrounding Bhutan were another color. The image remained still and scannable. I moved my eyes and scanned the map. I saw a wordless map of a country with roughly twenty districts clearly outlined (not much like the true map of Bhutan, although I did not notice that). I no longer saw my left hand within the image.

I turned my eyes to the upper left of the map, which was now pink, and saw in the northwest district of the country three small curved parallel lines. I looked to the right, putting the northwest area out of sight. When I looked back to the northwest, the outline of the district was still there and looked the same, but now the three lines within it were a bit larger. I looked to the right and back again. This time, the three lines were even larger and lower down within the same district. Then the complete image faded away.

From dreaming to lying awake, there had been a continuity of visual image, seeing, and scanning. Although the visual image continued from the dream, dreamed body imagery was lost as I became aware of my body lying in bed. Visual dream imagery had become scannable hypnopompic imagery, but not geometric. Because my eyes were still closed, I experienced the image as located within the awareness of my head.

The image of the two-dimensional page had no look of relative depth, but I saw and scanned the stilled image just as I see and scan a wide book page when awake and just as I scan lattice imagery when it fills the visual surface. I did not remember seeing any crease between two pages, as one would see with an open book, either during the dream or when I later saw the image. As with lattice imagery, it was impossible to move my eyes without scanning the image and thus scanning the map. This means that the map was located in a fixed position within the confines of the scannable visual surface. My view of the page changed in strict coordination with my eye movement. At the same time, my eyes moved up and down and to the sides as they would during perception, giving the effect of looking in various directions. It was as though I were perceiving in the waking manner. Yet, my eyes were closed.

As I scanned the image, the part that I put off screen for a while always appeared again when I scanned back toward it, just as happens with lattice imagery. As with lattices, I think of what is off screen at any time as potential image only. I consider that a visual image is visual only while I see it. This experience suggests that, during ordinary dreaming, dream-related potential imagery may lie beyond the visual field, either in spatial continuity from what was seen previously, or even as something potentially new (as were the changing parallel lines). So although, visually speaking, there may be to a dream only what I see at any moment, a little more potential image may lie outside the dream visual field within the limits of the visual surface, waiting (in a sense) to become image as I scan or even changing as I scan.

36. Dream Reality

The most obvious characteristic of dreams is that they simulate waking experience. I dreamed I walked into the room and found the tea laborers gathered there, and we sang. The people and the singing were simulations of what I might see and hear if I were awake. It is the simulation that makes the dream "only a dream." However, dreams contain more than simulations.

For example, my emotional feelings in a dream are not simulations of emotion and my reaction to what I see is not a simulation of a reaction. I really am aware of the dream narrative. My awareness is not a simulation of awareness. I really think, know, and understand as I dream, although I am limited in my memory and mental abilities, even during lucid dreaming. When we stopped singing "Amazing Grace," I thought about what to do next. My thinking was not a simulation of thinking. I may think and understand something that is not so, but I really "think" it and "understand" it within the context and limitations of the dream.

Indeed, if I feel afraid, although what I am afraid of is not physically there, I really feel afraid. If I feel relief in the dream, I really feel relief. If in a dream I see a German shepherd dog, I do not, as in waking life, perceive a flesh and blood dog, but I do literally see the image of the dog, just as I do when I am awake, and I feel wary. When I believe the dog may bite me, I really believe that. Sometimes, the emotional feelings continue after I wake up, after all simulation has stopped.

Although imagery largely simulates, the imagery itself is really there. Green is green and not a simulation of green. Light is really light and no different from when I am awake. If I hear the tea laborers singing "Amazing Grace," no one is there singing, but the visual image of the people and the sound of their singing is really present to me. Our singing is a true event, and for me it is an authentic time of worship, simulation and all.

When, while dreaming, I feel tingling, dizziness, or pain, or feel myself leaning back in my restaurant chair with my eyes closed, it is a real experience, even though I have no solid three-dimensional dream body or solid dream chair holding me up. Although the laws of physics are gone, the laws of how dreams work and how I see visual imagery are really functioning. Imagery disappears and may not appear again. Colors and forms change without consistency. I can walk on air, fly, or float and I can close my dreamed eyes to concentrate my attention on the darkness. I can really move my eyes to look at the image of Charlotte or to look directly toward the sun in the middle of the light. I can scan what I see. How can that be said not to happen?

I also have some control over what I do. I watch the singers to see whether the movement of their mouths is coordinated with their singing. After we sing, I plan what to do next and decide that there is probably not enough time to say the Lord's Prayer. I look toward the sun that appears high in the visual field. At the level of imagery, the dream actually happens and I act within it. The body imagery that I direct to move is only dream imagery, but, to the extent that I have some free will when I dream, or even if I am compelled to do so, I do direct the body imagery and see and feel my body image move accordingly, just as I do when I am awake. If I react to the image of the dog by running, I really make my body imagery run and I feel myself running as much as I do when I run while awake. If, in a dream, I direct my attention to a doorway or to Patty's painting on the wall, I actually do so. If I close my (dreamed) eyes to concentrate on the darkness, I really do so. Waking up does not eliminate my having done all that.

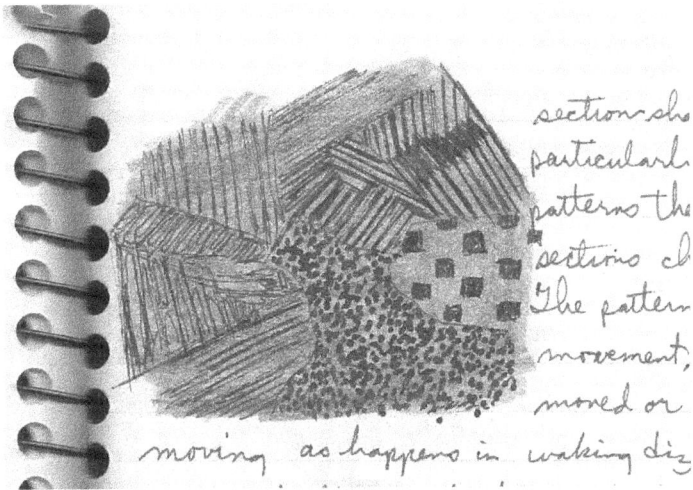

Figure 4. Part of a jumble of patterns that I saw in the dark once after closing my eyes while dreaming, as sketched in my notebook.

37. Patterns in the Dark

To eliminate visual dream imagery I usually just close my eyes in the dream. When I do that, I simply see darkness. Rarely, I have seen some other image along with the darkness, as when I saw a disk of light off to my left. On one unique occasion, I saw a jumble of patterns.

> I dreamed (January 28, 1987) that I was in my grand-mother's kitchen. I went to the door to the pantry to look, when it felt like someone gave a strong tug down on my lungi (my Indian clothing), but I saw no one near me. I realized I was dreaming. Through habit, I closed my (dreamed) eyes, and my visual field became dark. While I looked left and right within the darkness, I lost my feeling of standing on the floor and floated up. I began to toss about, shooting feet forward every which way with great force. Nevertheless, I kept my attention on the darkness before me.
>
> Finally I discerned in the darkness a faint jumble of patterns divided into irregularly-shaped sections (see Figure 4, from a sketch in my notebook). I noticed no relationship between what I saw and the preceding dream. Each section had some kind of agitation within it that did not change the pattern. In spite of my tossing about, the patterns remained as though in front of me and scannable, which means that they were in a fixed location within the visual surface. My attention remained most of the time on one section of the whole, which is the part that I tried to sketch. The patterns did not move in coordination with my dreamed body movement, although at times there seemed to be some visual jerking to the left, as when I feel dizzy while awake. Whether there were some gradual changes in the boundaries of the sections, I cannot say.
>
> There were eight to twelve irregular sections, whose patterns reached to the edges of the neighboring sections.

Most of the sections contained a striped or herringbone pattern, one looked granular, and one had a chessboard pattern. It all looked like imagery that I had seen before along with lattice imagery. Since the visual field was dark, the contrasts within the patterns were only between grays or gray and black. There was some agitation within the patterns that might be called glittering if it had been brighter. It seemed I would not have noticed the patterns except that I had decided to examine the darkness. The patterns were geometric imagery, not dream imagery. Only I was still dreaming bodily and not aware of my bed or bedroom.

When I woke up and became aware of my body in bed, the patterns continued without a break, but became even dimmer. I still felt tingly, and possibly dizzy, from tossing around in the dream. I was still able to scan the patterns for what seemed like 20 seconds longer. There was very little light in my room. My waking scanning of the patterns was in continuity from and subjectively no different from my scanning them while dreaming and was similar to my usual scanning of lattice imagery.

This type of jumbled pattern was not too different from imagery illustrated by Shepard (1978). Shepard experienced his imagery only by putting pressure on his eyeballs. Shepard was awake when he saw his imagery. I might say that while asleep I was dreaming bodily, but not visually.

The patterns that I saw in the darkness did not appear to have any obvious relationship to the darkness. However, it is clear that what we see as darkness can sometimes have an "undercurrent" of elementary imagery, not exactly not seen, but unnoticed.

38. Breaking Things Up

In contrast to the dark patterns that I described in the last section, I will tell of a different kind of experience. I had decided that, when I try to eliminate dream imagery in order to create dreamless sleep, the step of closing my eyes before concentrating on an imagined flame was theoretically not necessary. For, I thought, if I were to concentrate on an imagined flame without closing my eyes, any visual dream imagery would still be eliminated automatically through being ignored. I reasoned that closing my eyes had simply been a shortcut in the procedure. I would try to eliminate the dream imagery by concentrating on a flame without closing my eyes. In a dream recorded on August 25, 1981:

> I had been walking from room to room and building to building for a long time. I remembered that I frequently do that in a dream and thereupon realized I was dreaming. Without stopping my walking or closing my (dreamed) eyes, I began to concentrate my attention on an imagined flame. I did not produce a flame to see. At first I still saw the dream room that I was in, but the room quickly broke apart and what I saw did not become a dark visual field but continued to look like the visual imagery breaking apart. I lost the floor from under me, as often happens when I concentrate on something.
>
> The broken-up visual image filled the visual field and changed constantly, until it looked like quickly moving lattice imagery, which it may or may not have been precisely. I tried to concentrate on what I saw, but what I saw kept moving and changing. Being utterly distracted by the quickly moving patterns, I briefly studied them to the extent I could, but then I thought I should try again to concentrate. However, I could not keep my attention on anything either imagined or seen. There was too much rapid change.

With my perceptual mindset, I felt that I was tossed about within the patterns. The patterns filled the visual field and seemed to quickly pass on all sides of me, coming toward me and passing below me and then coming as if from below me, making me feel that I was passing rapidly backward and forward and then turning and tossing about in no particular order. My body movement remained coordinated with the moving of the imagery. The experience continued until I woke up.

Afterward, as I thought about what I had seen and felt, I reasoned that, because I had neither closed my eyes nor looked off into space, I had not eliminated the scene that I was within. I had just broken up the scene into geometric imagery. The imagery seemed to be quickly-shifting lattices, but whatever the imagery was it had sped by too quickly for me to inspect it closely. In any case, the imagery appeared to move as a whole, and not with pieces moving every-which-way. The direction of its movement across the visual field changed often and suddenly in no apparently consistent way. My experience appears to be comparable to reported drug-induced geometric hallucinations that occur when body imagery shares in the hallucination (as in Siegel, 1977; Siegel & Jarvik, 1975). Kenneth Moss (1985a, 1985b) also reports creating moving elementary imagery while manipulating lucid dreaming.

I can understand a little better now what was happening with the visual imagery, in terms of the perceptual mindset and the hemispheric projection. With the projection forward of the hemisphere, I saw the moving imagery as surrounding me. In this case, I was tossing about within a dome of moving lattices or possibly broken lattices, with my viewpoint being at the center of the base of the hemisphere. The moving forms were passing through the whole elementary visual field, as if above me and below me and farther back on both sides of me, passing by the sides of my head, and above and below the perceptual visual field—where I don't see anything while awake. The tossing imagery, although rapid, was all evenly bright, clear, and precise in detail, in contrast to my seeing during perception, as far as I could tell.

As any imagery moved toward any part of the boundary of the visual field, I saw it as moving from in front of me to passing by me to behind me, and it made me feel that I was being projected toward what I saw in the center of the visual field. When imagery moved from the boundary toward the center, it appeared to be coming from behind me to in front of me and made me feel that I was being moved away from what I saw or backwards. So that any imagery that moved quickly from one edge of the visual field to its opposite produced the effect of my spinning or tossing about rapidly.

I could see no regularity in the direction of movement of the imagery or my movement although the speed of the movement seemed to remain constant. Because the normal distortion of lattice imagery is greater in the outer areas of the hemisphere, the imagery seemed to move more quickly through the outer reaches than it did when it passed through the center of the visual field. Therefore, the pattern looks like it slows down as it approaches the center of the visual field and speeds up again more and more as it crosses the opposite half of the visual field.

Of course, there was no dream world to break up beyond the imagery itself. If I had closed my (dreamed) eyes when I realized I was dreaming, I would have given the visual part of my dream world a more gentle finality.

The breaking up of the dream into elementary imagery is the opposite of the image-making process seen in the taking of drugs. When drugs are taken, the geometrical and other elementary imagery are seen first. Then "the elementary forms of the first stage seem to combine with 'complex' images, which eventually may replace the forms in the second stage" (Siegel & Jarvik, 1975, p. 111). Complex imagery would include such things as landscapes, faces, and familiar objects. With drugs, elementary imagery transitions to complex imagery. As I understand it, when I continued looking at the image instead of eliminating it by closing my eyes, I reversed the process of hallucination formation and was in the process of changing the complex dream imagery back to elementary forms.

There certainly was a wow factor to this experience, but no spirituality. The excitement was extremely kinesthetic and not numinous.

39. Entanglements

Lucid dreaming came to me spontaneously. I knew nothing about such dreams beforehand and I had lucid dreams over a period of almost two years before I heard that I was not the only person to have such dreams. Some people have tried to start having lucid dreams, and there are books and articles that help people to do this. However, it was not as though I had heard of lucid dreaming and tried to have lucid dreams at the expense of ordinary dreams. I recognize the value of ordinary dreams. I know that sometimes when I come to know I am dreaming I have unintentionally interrupted what might otherwise have become a valuable dream. However, I find that once I am lucid, the innocence of nonlucid dreaming is gone and not to be recovered, except, perhaps, by forgetting that I am dreaming, which has happened only rarely.

Sometimes when I come to know I am dreaming, the dream even shows me that I should not interrupt what is happening. For example:

I realized I was dreaming, so I wanted to fly off into the sky, perhaps with some notion of eliminating dream imagery. I flew into the air. Then I heard a dog barking. I saw a small brown dog running around below on the ground barking and barking at me. It distracted me greatly. I stayed in the air trying to outlast the barking, but the dog wouldn't stop. Finally I decided that the dog had to be taken care of. So I

flew down to the dog and gave him a good hug, whereupon he was satisfied and stopped barking.

In this dream, I believed that I could not proceed with any
intentions of my own until the immediate demands of the
dream were met. Whatever the metaphorical value of the dog
was, I felt that I was not to disregard it. I think of such inter-
ferences as entanglements. My entanglement seemed to have a
purpose.

Another kind of entanglement that happened to me more
than once is that when I flew up in the air, either to eliminate
dream imagery or by habit, I would get entangled in some
telephone or electrical wires, such as run along the street from
pole to pole. I need to recognize when the demands of the
dream come first. Actually, whenever I realized I was dreaming, entanglements were the exception rather than the rule,
perhaps because in the more entangling dreams I do not tend
to become lucid.

While a dream may have a purpose that I should not ignore,
being lucid in a dream may also have a purpose that I should
not ignore, especially since lucid dreams came to me quite
naturally, like a gift. I do not assume that one type of dreaming
is to be preferred over the other. However, I do suspect that
sometimes people who have heard of lucid dreams and want to
produce them for whatever reason may not be ready to move
from ordinary dreaming to lucid dreaming. In which case, I
would expect entanglements to be common.

V

Light

40. Darkness and Light

When I see, whether I am awake or asleep, all that I see is color and visual form. By "color," I mean any hue that appears within my visual field, including black, white, varieties of gray, darkness, and light. Without color, there is no seeing. When I am awake with my eyes open, it looks like the colors I see, including darkness and light, belong to the surfaces and substances of the world that lies around me. I think, "My shirt has gray and white stripes." "I have an orange cat." But the colors are in the visual image, and are not external to my eyes. Nor is the darkness or brightness that I see ever "out there" in front of the eyes. I think, "I see light way over there." "The church is full of light." "Andy can't read in the bedroom, because he's lying in the dark."

However, darkness and light are not "out there." Those who study the eyes, retinas, and the visual cortex tell us that colors, the "stuff" of visual images, do not belong to the world that I see. The surfaces of the world have no color. Surfaces absorb some wavelengths of light and reflect others (Hubel, 1988; Nassau, 1980). The colors that I see during visual perception are determined by the dominant wavelengths of light that are received by the retina and by the brain's use of the incoming information (Hubel, 1988; Nassau, 1980; Nathans, 1989). Therefore, the mass of colors that I see cannot be an internal representation of external colors. The external world has no appearance, except when portrayed internally through colors. When I see the bright sun or the reflection of light off the roof, so to speak, the brightness that I see belongs to my visual field. Just as blueberries have no flavor until they are eaten, they have no color until they are seen.

Darkness is the absence of visual imagery, but it is also seen. When I see darkness, I do not see nothing. Seeing nothing would be the absence of darkness, light, and all manner of colors. David H. Hubel says that when he sees nothing during a visual migraine aura, he sees "literally, nothing—not white, grey, or black, but just what I see directly behind—nothing" (1988, p. 100). When there is only darkness within the perceptual visual field, neither light that travels to the retina nor unconscious processes are creating visual imagery. When I see darkness, I do not exactly see black. When I close my eyes, the darkness that I see is more like dark gray with areas of pale light or little specks of light. The intensity of the darkness can also change as when I close my eyes and then, after that, place my hands over my eyes.

When I walk by a house at night, I may say "I see the light on in Becky's living room," and it seems I see both the inside of the house and the light that reveals the inside of the house. It is natural to think of light from the lamps as three-dimensional stuff that fills the living room. However, I see only the forms within the house, depicted in color in various intensities. I see the forms, because light of various wavelengths is reflected from the surfaces of the rooms in the house and the light waves reach my eyes and cause my visual version of the house to have a bright living room. However, there is no brightness in the room apart from the colored forms that I see. I do not see the light waves in the house or some stuff called "light." I see the end product of the light waves that have reached my eyes, after my brain has done its work with the information brought to my eyes. When light waves to the eyes are intense enough, I "see light."

Brightness is an intensity of color. In everyday perception that intensity often adds all-color white to what I see, because light coming from the sun that "shines" on things produces the full spectrum of colors, which add up to white. When the intensity of color is so much that it begins to obscure the forms of the image, as when the sun gets in my eyes, I see less clearly the forms that represent the world. Even though brightness, like color and darkness, does not belong to the world, it tells me something about what is happening in the world.

When I am awake, no apparent harm comes from believing that the colors and brightness that I see belong to the world. The colors in their forms do reveal, or at least suggest closely, the shapes, sizes, boundaries, distances, textures, edges, and the spatial relationships of the things I see around me along with their relative movements and my own movements. The colors help me to distinguish one thing from another. The colors that I see might also tell me about the wavelengths of light coming to the eye or about molecules in the reflecting surfaces, if I knew enough science, but that is not very useful information for everyday life.

All visual imagery is the seeing of light, in the sense that all image creates a contrast with darkness. Brightness is the intensity of image. All visual imagery, including a visual field of intense brightness, I will see with a perceptual mindset, unless, perchance, I manage to see the visual field as a whole without looking at a particular part. With a visual field of darkness, I am usually aware that my eyes are shut, and I know that what I see is within my head. In any case, I do not seem to project the darkness forward, and there is no image to place at a distance.

41. Stable Intense Lights

In the "Amazing Grace" experience (section 1), the "sun" appeared high in front of me as my visual field filled with intense light. That experience is an example of the category of light that I call "stable intense lights." Stable intense lights are different from all other varieties of light imagery and have been of five kinds:

1. *The area of light* is an area of plain, uniform whiteness totally within view. It has a definite boundary, but does not have a recognizable shape. It appears like a gap within the dream scene or within darkness.

> I dreamed (April 13, 1983) that we were riding along a street in a car, when I recognized one of my students from the college in Jorhat walking along the street. I remembered that he had died. I thought this was remarkable and told the others in the car to look carefully as we passed him. I slowly realized that I was dreaming. As I thought about this being a dream, I felt myself rise up head first through the top of the car and out. I saw nothing around me. Then I felt I might be waking up and I began to sink. As I resisted waking up, I rose up again, and I was in darkness.
>
> Then I saw a light to the upper right of my head. It was neither a sun nor a disk of light. It was an area of light of no identifiable shape. I remembered to think of God (as planned when awake) and the light remained, but did not increase. I thought of God for some time. When I woke up and opened my eyes, my impression was that the light remained briefly in the same scannable spatial relationship to my eyes that it had been during the dream. When I say "scannable," I mean at least that I could turn my eyes to look toward it and look away from it, while it remained fixed in location. I could not place it in the center of the visual field because it was too near the boundary of the visual surface.

2. *The disk of light* appears as a perfectly round intensely white, but not vibrant, light with a well-defined circumference. There

are no marks within it, meaning that it is of uniform appearance across the disk. I have described earlier the disk of light that appeared once in the darkness to the left of my point of concentration (section 10). The area of light and the disk of light have the same appearance of uniform whiteness, with the disk of light looking like a brightly lit frosted light bulb or globe of light shining within the dark of night. In each of five cases, the disk of light has been surrounded by darkness because I had first closed my eyes within the dream and created darkness. Its size has varied from just larger than a star to much larger than what a full moon looks like. When first seen, the disk can be taken to be a sphere, but upon closer analysis, I see no shadings or signs that would indicate it is spherical (or that it is intended to look like it is) or three-dimensional. Nor does it have the subtle shadings of the moon. I now know that the image of the disk, like all visual imagery, is actually flat, because it appears on the flat visual field.

Disks of light have been reported by others in nonlucid and lucid dreams (Garfield, 1979; Sparrow, 1976, 1991), in night experiences while one is not fully asleep (Gackenbach, 1992–93; Gillespie, 2000; Woolman, 1971), Theravada Buddhist meditation (King, 1980), Hindu meditation (Sivananda, 1975), and in Christian mysticism (Matus, 1984). Whether any of these examples have all the characteristics of stable intense lights in addition to being disk-shaped is impossible for me to know from the descriptions given by the various writers.

3. *Peripheral light* is an intense light noticed on the periphery of the elementary visual field. If I turn my eyes toward the light, I may see that the light actually lies on the edge of the visual surface. I can know that, because when the light lies there, I cannot place the light in the center of the visual field. In any case, its intensity does not (ever? usually?) intrude into the perceptual visual field. The light may appear with or without an accompanying dream scene. In contrast with the frosted light-bulb whiteness of the area of light and disk of light, the

peripheral light has the vibrant intensity (or greater) of the perceptual sun.

> I dreamed (May 9, 1982) that Charlotte and I were walking closely together. She was to my left. It was night. I explained to her that every night I leave the world and go to a different place. I became aware of an intense light to my left that actually seemed to be located in the left corner of my left eye. I knew I was dreaming and remembered that seeing a light does not necessarily mean that I am waking up. I said to Charlotte, in so many words, "This is a dream and I have to experiment. Excuse me a minute." Then I kissed her on the cheek and walked off to my right to avoid the light. However, as I walked on, the light remained to my left. I could not turn away from it.
>
> The explanation might be that I was only turning my body away and not trying to turn my eyes away. Turning only my body would not change the position of the light within the visual field. Moving my eyes would influence the location of the light within the visual field or move it outside of the visual field. I could still see the dream scene vaguely in the rest of the visual field, although in this dream it was nighttime.

When peripheral light does not appear alongside a dream scene, it is accompanied by darkness. Sometimes, particularly when it appears at the top of the visual field, it immediately precedes another light event, such as the fullness of light.

4. *The sun-like concentration of light* is a round and bright light roughly like the perceptual experience of the sun. The sun-like light is also a disk, but it is much more intense and vibrant than what I call the disk of light, just as in everyday experience the perceptual sun is considerably brighter and more vibrantly alive than a bright light bulb or the perceptual full moon. The sun-like light appears in various sizes and is at times smaller or

larger than my experience of the perceptual sun. Sometimes the circumference of the sun is precisely defined and at other times the circumference is discernible but blurred. Not so commonly, several suns appear in a scannable group together or there are rays connected to the sun.

> I dreamed (May 19, 1983) that I was in a tailoring shop in New York City looking up at the walls and ceiling. I went into the air to look at things more closely. My attention never went back to the lower part of the room. I was thinking, "Oh, this is exactly how walls look [traditionally] in Assam." Then I realized from my being in the air that I was dreaming. I did not think to close my eyes or concentrate in order to experiment, as was my custom at that time. I wanted to spin around. I began spinning around, calling "Jesus" over and over. I noticed that there was a sun high within the visual field. I continued to spin around, changing my cry to "God." Soon there appeared a cluster of six or seven very bright suns before my eyes. As I spun like a top, all I saw were the suns and the light around them, including a confusion of rays. I thought that it was my spinning around that made the sun multiply. In spite of my spinning, the suns remained in a fixed scannable location as a group in front of my eyes and in a stable spatial relationship with each other. They did not change or move as I looked from one to another and studied them. I felt a rope tangle with my ankle as I turned. I had trouble with the rope more than once. I woke up.

Experiences of a sun-like light are sometimes reported by others in meditation, mystical experience, or lucid dreaming (e.g. Eliade, 1962/1965; Matus, 1984; Sivananda, 1975; Sparrow, (1976); Symeon the New Theologian, 1980), but it is impossible to know from the reports in which cases the sun might have any of the other characteristics of the stable intense lights. To give an example from someone else's story and to show some variety, I quote here from Symeon the New Theologian, whose experiences tend to remind me of my own.

I had frequently seen a light, at times within, when my soul had enjoyed calmness and peace. At times it appeared to me externally, from afar, or even it was completely hidden, and by its hiddenness caused me the unbearable pain of thinking I would not see it again. But when I lamented and wept and displayed complete solitude and humility it appeared to me again. It was like the sun as it penetrates through the thickness of the mist and gradually shows itself a gently glowing sphere. Thus Thou, the ineffable, the invisible, the impalpable, the immovable, who always art everywhere present in all things and fillest everything, at all times, or if I may say so, by day and by night, art seen and art hidden. ... Thou who art everywhere present art suddenly found and manifested like another sun. O ineffable condescension. (Symeon, 1980, pp. 364–365)

5. *The fullness of light* is a vibrant, intense light with a boiling effect, filling the elementary visual field and appearing to surround me, as I described in my experiences of the fullness, such as when I called "Father," and in the "Amazing Grace" experience. The fullness is customarily accompanied by deep devotional feelings and uncontrollable joy and reverence in addition to the knowledge that God is present. Nevertheless, on the first occasion of the fullness, it was as though I woke up before the experience became as intense as in later experiences. In all 13 experiences that I include in this category, except the first time, I saw a "sun" within the vibrancy of the visual field. The sun within the fullness of light is a form of the "sun-like concentration of light." However, with the fullness, the sun itself tends to be a little less intense than the rest of the visual field. It is the usual stable and scannable presence of the sun

within the bright visual field of the fullness that confirms that the fullness of light belongs to the category of stable intense lights.

42. Lights Beyond Dreaming

The common characteristics of stable intense lights differentiate them from all other forms of light imagery. In fact, all the characteristics that I present here make it clear that stable intense lights are not dream imagery. I think of them as lying beyond dreaming.

1. *They remain at a fixed location within the visual surface.* Even though I am dreaming, a stable intense light does not move from its fixed location within the visual surface and it is scannable, just as lattice imagery or the stilled dream image is scannable.

2. *They are not integrated with the dream.* Because the light's location within the visual surface remains fixed, it cannot be integrated with any dreamed visual or body imagery that may accompany it. Unlike the usual dream imagery, it does not move into and out of my visual field in coordination with my dreamed movement, as when I spin or dance. Usually in a dream, if I turn or spin to my left, the visual image of anything will move to my right, simulating what happens when I am awake. However, when I see a stable intense light, my movement is dreamed, but the light remains in place before my eyes, so to speak. Sometimes some visual dream imagery will be in harmony with my movement, but the light is not.

I have mentioned that when I dream there is no three-dimensional dreamed body of any sort. There is only the subjective body experience, which is all that is needed for simulating waking experience. My visual field, where all my seeing of color and visual form happens, remains, as always, between the left and right sides of my sleeping head. So that, even when visual dream imagery acts appropriately like perceptual imagery, by changing spatially in coordination with my dreamed movement, my image of a stable intense light remains scannable between the left and right sides of my sleeping head. So that, even when I spin around or dance, the image of light remains visible "before my eyes." The light does not leave my sight.

3. *They are not representational.* Dream imagery simulates my seeing the things of everyday life, either normally or in a bizarre fashion. That is, it is representational. However, a stable intense light does not appear to represent anything beyond itself. It plays no part in dream simulation. It is an image of light, so that it doesn't shine on anything. Peripheral light does not appear to represent anything that I am familiar with nor anything that I can normally see. The area of light looks like a hole in the visual field. It is common for me to think of a stable intense light, when I see it, as simply "a light" or "the light." In one sense, light does not represent light because, like all image, it *is* light to begin with, whether it represents perceived light or not. It might have form and represent something else in ordinary dreams, such as a street light or a lit up window. However, a stable intense light is just being itself.

Although the disk of light may appear like a spotless moon, or the "sun" may be taken for a sun, either disk may look too small or too large to really represent a moon or sun, and most often the form appears in front of me, not as though above in the sky. Stable intense lights show no perspective. They are not represented as shining on anything or causing shadows.

Rudolf Arnheim (1969) has noted that the circle, like the sun or the moon, is the simplest natural shape. It is commonly found in the natural world. It makes sense to me to understand the disk and "sun" of stable intense lights as simply fitting into the prevalence of circles in visual experience and in biology itself, apart from the representation of sun or moon. I think of the circumference of the elementary visual field or of the visual surface, the eyeball itself, the fovea in the center of the retina, the projected hemisphere of vision, and the circle that a single bubble presents sitting on the surface of water. In hypnopompic imagery, there have been the rows of circles in lattices. Circles may be as natural to stable intense lights as squares are to lattice imagery.

4. *They sometimes appear outside the perceptual visual field.* Stable intense lights may appear anywhere within the elementary visual field. Dreams as a rule simulate perceptual experience, so that the dream visual field is not likely to extend beyond the perceptual visual field. In fact, my dream imagery sometimes seems not even to fill what would be the perceptual visual field, but tends to stay near the center, where my attention is directed. The peripheral light that I saw when I kissed Charlotte and walked off to my right stayed a bit too far to the left to look like it belonged to the dream scene in any normal way. It was located beyond the limits of the perceptual visual field. Therefore, I understood it to be in the left corner of my left eye. Nothing else made sense.

Likewise, the light of the fullness fills the elementary visual field, not just the perceptual visual field. Therefore, its outer areas lie in directions from the eye where I do not usually see anything. The fact that stable intense lights are not limited to the perceptual visual field suggests that they are best classed with elementary imagery.

5. *The same form of light may appear during different dreams at the same location within the visual surface.* For example, in the five times that the peripheral light accompanied a scene, it appeared four times as though in the left corner of my left eye. In four of the 13 cases that I considered to be the fullness of light, I saw first an intense peripheral light, high above the perceptual visual field. I don't think I ever saw it actually move from the top to lower down in the visual field. Probably a light first appeared above and then a light appeared below, but it looked like the first light moved down. Areas of light tended to appear half-way down just to the left of the center of the visual

surface. My conclusion is that certain areas of my visual surface are prone to certain stable intense light manifestations, given the right circumstances. I cannot be more specific about what the right circumstances would be.

6. *They may remain visible after I wake up.* Rarely, I continue to see, without a break, the light in the same location within the visual surface after I awaken, and I can continue to look at it, that is, scan it and look away from it for a while.

These characteristics of stable intense lights all demonstrate that they are not dream imagery. The fullness of light, like all stable intense lights, may interrupt a dream or be in continuity from a dream, but these light forms themselves clearly lie beyond the dream image-making process. The fullness of light is not itself a dream experience, although it has certainly appeared in continuity from dreaming. In the same manner, body experience during the fullness of light, though it is in continuity from normal dreamed body experience, passes beyond normal experience into flying, floating, and the gradual disappearance of body awareness.

43. The Six Yogas of Naropa

My experiences of the fullness of light occurred from 1981 to 1985. Even after the last of these, I still thought of the dreamless sleep that I had been looking for primarily in the context of Hinduism and the Upanishads. I was slow to realize that the teachings about lucid dreaming and dreamless sleep in the Tibetan Tantric Buddhist tradition known as the Six Yogas of Naropa were more likely relevant to my experiences, at least on the subjects of lucid dreaming and light, than was the discussion in the Upanishads. Gradually, more books, with much more information on Naropa's teaching about lucid dreaming, became available in English.

The Tibetan discussions date from as early as the eleventh century CE, when the Indian Buddhist teacher, Naropa, passed on the teachings to his Tibetan pupil, Marpa (Dowman, 1985; Guenther, 1963; Heruka, 1982; Tucci, 1970/1980; Young, 1999). In India, the teachings originated centuries before that, a notable source of the teaching being the *Guhyasamājatantra*, dated probably in the third century CE (Bhattacharya, 1967).

The Six Yogas of Naropa mention Buddhist tantric meditation in three contexts: while one is awake, while asleep, and after death. The teachings are certainly much more complex than I can present them here. According to the teachings, the aim of meditation is to gain control over the energies of the body and in the end to find liberation from repeated rebirths. They include teaching on how to enter meditation immediately upon falling asleep or during lucid dreaming. Sleep meditation, either upon falling asleep or within lucid dreaming, includes the visualization of traditional Buddhist imagery. This meditation is thought of as dream yoga. When successful, meditation leads to a variety of experiences of the Void, which is the emptiness that is believed to underlie all existence. These experiences of the Void lead eventually to the clear light of the Void and liberation. The early followers of the teaching did not intend to share their knowledge with the general public. They composed the texts for a restricted number of yogis within certain Tibetan Buddhist traditions.

The texts describe the eight signs of dreamless sleep that appear in a sequence when sleep meditation is properly done. The signs of dreamless sleep are discussed only in terms of the visual, and certain texts make it clear that the signs are literally seen (Gyatso, 1982; Tsongkhapa, 1996, 1997; Wayman, 1977). These signs show the progression from dream to dreamless sleep. They are not only signs that one has achieved dreamless sleep, but some sources mention that they indicate one's progress in the dissolution of the elements of the body and of consciousness.

The eight visual signs are described in terms of light and darkness. The first four visions are minor signs, usually described as a mirage-like appearance, smoke-like appearance, sparkling lights like fireflies at night, and then the appearance of a steady lamplight. The four visions that follow the minor signs are signs of the Void that underlies all things. First there is seen a clear, bright, moonlit sky. Next, there is glowing sunlight. The third sign has two phases: the first is a vision like a very dark empty sky, then there is deep unconsciousness. This is the deepest of dreamless sleep. The last sign is the clear light of the Void, which has been described by Tsongkhapa, a prominent commentator on the Six Yogas, as "of a color like the blending of the lights of sun and moon in a sky free from all darkness, like the clear sky at early dawn" (1997, p. 130). This clear light, when retained, leads to liberation.

Although the visions are described in terms of smoke, fireflies, skies, and such, they are not thought of as dreams of smoke, fireflies, and skies. This is what the imagery looks like when sleeping vision becomes dreamless. There is allowance for variety in the sequence. It is said that the same eight signs of sleep are achievable during daytime meditation and are always seen upon dying. Tsongkhapa explains that one's ability in meditation in the waking state helps meditation during sleep, and helps one through the process of dying and rebirth. You may notice that this Tibetan description of the experiences of dreamless sleep does not match the earlier discussion of dreamless sleep in the Upanishads.

To achieve the clear light of the Void through sleep and dream yoga is not a simple work at all. To give only a taste of Tibetan discussions of dream yoga, the following is a part of Tsongkhapa's description of what one does while dreaming:

> This stage of the practice can only be undertaken when the training in retaining conscious presence during dreams has become stable. Here meditate upon yourself as the manifest radiant form of the mandala deity. The mantric syllable HUM shines with a great light from your heart. This light

melts the animate and inanimate dream objects into light, which is absorbed into yourself. Your body then also melts into light, from the head downward and feet upward, and is absorbed into the HUM at your heart. The HUM then melts into unapprehendable clear light. Rest the mind unwaveringly within this light. (Tsongkhapa, 1997, p. 128)

Certainly there are serious limits in comparing Tibetan Buddhist practices with either Christian mysticism or secular Western writing on lucid dreaming. The Tibetan teaching is thoroughly mixed with traditional Buddhist metaphysics and religion and is based upon an esoteric understanding of the body. Serinity Young (1999), who has written about Tibetan dream practices and is well aware of the Western interest in lucid dreaming, warns about easy comparisons between Tibetan dream yoga and the Western understanding and use of lucid dreaming. She stresses the differences between the two traditions in cultural and religious contexts, dream content, goals of lucid dreaming, and practices within the dream.

Nevertheless, I came to understand that the visual signs of dreamless sleep as described in the Tibetan texts are not dream imagery, just as my stable intense lights, including the disk of light, the sun-like light, and the fullness of light, are not dream imagery, although I am asleep. It seems that my efforts at the elimination of dreaming, my concentration of attention on the darkness, and my religious mindset (both conscious and, I believe, unconscious) in lucid dreams that led to the fullness of light, though essentially different from practices described in the Six Yogas, nevertheless seem to parallel somehow the Tibetan practices in ways that are not clear to me.

I find in my own experiences of stable intense lights and darkness a general confirmation of the Tibetan discussions of the visual phenomena that they associate with dreamless sleep. I say only a "general confirmation," because I do not see any confirmation that my experiences of light match up specifically to any of theirs. In any case, it is hard to tell. The Tibetan discussions of the signs of dreamless sleep as literally seen also assure me that my own observations of the "dreamless" status of stable intense lights are not just unique personal experiences. I realize that I am only at the beginning of thinking through these matters.

It is also clear that the Void that the Tibetans find accessible beyond dreams and the experience of the presence of God that I have found in light are two different experiences, and their phenomenology cannot be the same. The disappearance of one's essential person into the "clear light of the Void," in the Buddhist manner, is not described as an experience of God. The Void is void of God. And the awareness of God's presence in light and being overcome with intense reverence and joy cannot be mistaken for having found any kind of Void. Nor do an experience of the light of the Void and an awareness of the presence of God in the light appear to lie in any kind of necessary phenomenological or ontological continuum, even though they may lie in some order of one's own preference.

44. Mandalas

For the Tantric Buddhists of Tibet, a mandala is an elaborately detailed, colorful image that is painted or at times constructed of colored sand. The mandala may also be memorized and created visually in the mind. The mandala is used primarily as an aid for meditation. In the Kalachakra mandala, the lotus seat of the presiding deity, Kalachakra, and his consort lies at the very center of the palace, which itself lies in the center of the mandala (Bryant, 1992). The presiding deity varies according to the tantric text that goes with the mandala.

Each mandala is painted or constructed in accordance with the description given in the text, which is called a Tantra. All details throughout the mandala focus on the deity. The palace of the deity in the center is square, with an elaborate gate on each of the four sides. The palace and the mandala in this way fall into a four-fold pattern. Large concentric circles surrounding the palace are filled with their own related illustrations. The mandala is most commonly shown in two-dimensional form with the view of the mandala being from above.

While the mandala represents the universe with the deity in the center, it also represents the initiate's or mystic's internal world, showing the journey that is to be taken to the center of the palace, where he or she is to visualize and become identified with the deity (Tucci, 1961). The Dalai Lama, in telling his own story, explained that part of his practice is deity yoga, "during which I use different *mandalas* to visualize myself as a succession of different 'deities.' (This should not, however, be taken to imply belief in independent external beings)" (Dalai Lama, 1990, p. 207). This visualization is part of the meditation centered on emptiness.

The mandalas of the Hindu Tantrics of India include some of the same basic characteristics as Tibetan mandalas, such as the outer border, circles, a square with a gate on each side, and a central focus on a deity or an equivalent, but they are simpler and more geometric forms, rather than pictorial. They commonly include triangles and Sanskrit mantras or syllables (Tucci, 1961).

C.G. Jung (1968, 1969a), aware of the Hindu and Tibetan Buddhist use of mandalas, gave the name "mandala" to a certain type of imagery that may appear spontaneously during dreams, visions, or active imagination. A Jungian mandala is a concentrically arranged pattern, within a square or a circle, in which the center signifies the psychic center of the personality. In the center, there may be a sun, a star, or a cross or something significant to the dreamer. Around the center, there is a four-way design, as in the Asian mandalas.

The mandala that appears in a dream may be seen as a scene, a picture, or a diagram, or it may be the setting in which the dream takes place, such as a city square or a temple. Or the dreamer's movements may form a square or a circle. In the center is found a representation of the self or wholeness. Jung felt that the appearance of a mandala in a dream or a vision, or during active imagination, indicates a rearranging of the personality, a reconciliation of differences between the conscious and unconscious sides of one's life, and a new psychological centering. Its appearance is commonly accompanied by numinosity, emotion, or a sense of significance.

There are some important differences between the Asian mandalas and Jungian mandalas. My focus is on the more elaborate Tibetan mandala. The construction of the Tibetan mandala admits no freedom or deviation from the descriptions in the tantric literature (Tucci, 1961). However, Jungian mandalas are not predetermined. They occur only spontaneously in dreams, visions, or active imagination, and thus seem to be "free creations of fantasy, but determined by certain archetypal ideas unknown to their creators" (Jung, 1969a, p. 360). Therefore, in Jungian mandalas we cannot expect to find the precision of required detail as found in the Asian mandalas.

Although the Hindu or Buddhist understanding of a mandala is religious, with its center signifying a palace in which a deity or equivalent is symbolized, Jung felt that:

> A modern mandala is an involuntary confession of a peculiar mental condition. There is no deity in the mandala, nor is there any submission or reconciliation to a deity. The place of the deity seems to be taken by the wholeness of man. (Jung, 1969b, p. 82)

Any dreams of mine that I consider to be mandala dreams are necessarily only Jungian-type mandalas, except that my God does not appear to have been replaced by "the wholeness of man." Two years before my first experience of the fullness of light, I dreamed:

I was being a Japanese priest and wore a long robe. I was in a large lacquered room whose dominant colors were red and black. The room was like the interior of a temple. Another priest came into the room with an object about eight inches high that I thought of as a five-sided abacus. The pattern on each side of the object was an alternation of red and black squares as on a chess board. It was a valuable thing, he said, which was not known to others. I put the instrument to my mouth, as one would put a megaphone to the mouth, and I marched slowly counterclockwise around the room in priestly fashion. I began to sing joyfully a Japanese song through the five-sided abacus.

I soon realized that I did not know Japanese and did not know the meaning of my words, but it did not matter. When I glanced out of a window that I was passing to my right, and thus looking away from the center of my circum-ambulation, I realized I was dreaming, but I was not tempted to leave my drama to experiment with dreaming, which had been my custom. What I was doing was important to me. After I finished singing, I left the room with the other priest to visit someone, to whom I planned to take a gift.

I consider this to be a mandala dream in the Jungian sense, at least in the sense that the center of the temple played a part. I circumambulated the center, but I did not yet reach the center. The experience was peaceful and felt significant.

I consider all my experiences of the fullness of light to be mandala dreams in the Jungian sense, with God positioned in the center. By that I mean that God was the center of the experience, and I was in the center, where I knew the presence of God. Some of my experiences of the fullness of light have more obviously developed out of mandala dreams. In the "Amazing Grace" dream (section 1), I was singing a hymn in the square room with the tea garden laborers. This was a significant room because of our worship. There was peace and joy even before the appearance of light. I was with a celestial choir of tea garden laborers singing praises around the throne of God, as I think of it. (This is a metaphor. No picture of a throne is intended here.) Then the singers all disappeared in light with the sudden presence of God coming into our midst. In another experience of the fullness, I danced in the middle of the large empty room while the light that was centered above me eliminated all other visual imagery (section 46).

The rooms in these two dreams became temples for me (or palaces of God, so to speak), and when the light appeared, I found God to be present. In other dreams, the center, that is, the light and the presence of God, seems to have just broken into my dreaming. Sometimes, I had only started to eliminate my dream environment when the light eliminated all other imagery, so I cannot know whether I would have experienced more specific mandala imagery. Jungian mandalas, as far as I can see, are much more loosely conceived than Asian mandalas, and I believe that my fullness of light experiences, where I found God and numinosity in the center, fit into the pattern of a Jungian mandala.

Because my hypnopompic lattice patterns are highly geometrical and regular, there may arise the question whether they can be considered mandala imagery. What is normally required for a mandala, whether Asian or Jungian, is that it at least have a clearly defined boundary, four-way symmetry or at least a four-way pattern, a focused center, and some degree of numinosity (Eliade, 1969; Jung, 1968, 1969a, 1969b; Snellgrove, 1987; Tucci, 1961).

My hypnopompic lattice patterns, whether chessboard, crisscross, or constructed of hexagons, have included no central figure or any image within the pattern identifiable as a center to which everything else is related or around which symmetry or a four-way pattern is organized. Instead, lattices are uniform across the visual field and the visual surface. It is the boundary of the visual field itself or the boundary of the visual surface that determines the limits of the image, and though every elementary visual field is round and contains the imagery, the boundary itself is neither a visual representation nor a symbol. Nor do I see in my lattices any four-way symmetry or any other four-way division of the pattern.

Finally and especially, although I am often impressed by my lattice imagery, when I see it, it is not an emotional, numinous, or significant experience for me. I may react with pleasure or interest, but I may also study the lattice image in a detached manner. I do not believe that the patterns qualify as Jungian mandalas, or Indian or Tibetan mandalas for that matter. I do believe that, due to the limited light coming through my eyelids, they are an activation of the elementary image-making properties of the visual field, when neither perceptual nor unconscious processes are producing anything more representational.

45. Light Only

A dream of May 30, 1992:

> I was walking near the river in Gauhati when I saw water overflowing the river bank. I was carrying a load of books and papers and had become lucid. I flew up over the river and turned toward the sun. As I looked toward the sun, I realized that I could drop my books and be free of them, and so I did. I felt devotional and called out over and over, "Jesus." I began to examine the sun. It was plain bright white, clearly defined, and slightly larger than an average sun in the sky. It did not have the vibrant or boiling look at all. The sky was probably brighter nearest to the sun. There was something like a mist partly over the sun, which would account for the lack of vibrancy. I continued to call Jesus. Then I woke up.

I did not consider this dream to be the fullness of light. Normally the decision to consider an experience to be the fullness has been a judgment I've had to make upon awaking. Sometimes during light covering the visual field, I feel at the time that I am having an experience of God, but my waking judgment later tells me not to classify that one as a fullness. Either the brightness of the visual field is not intense enough or not really throughout the visual field, or the religious part of the experience is not spontaneous and overwhelming enough. Sometimes there is more thrill than reverence. However, I believe that having light of some sort throughout the visual field is important enough to be a category of its own, which I call "light only."

The experience of the fullness of light is a distinct experience, but the fact that I have to make a waking judgment about where to draw the line between experiences of the fullness and those which seemed to be not quite their equal shows that there has been for me no clear boundary between the fullness and other experiences. Some experiences were unquestionably in every way the fullness of light, but if I were to look through all my reports of light only again, perhaps in a few cases I would determine differently now whether one or another qualified as the fullness of light. Perhaps there is not a recognizable boundary between knowing the presence of God and not knowing, but rather a question of relative nearness, so to speak. This takes more thinking and perhaps gets more analytical than is useful.

It seems to me that there is good reason to recognize a category called "light only." Light only includes all experiences of the fullness of light, all visual fields of light that include a sun, whether the sun is a stable intense light or not, and fields of light in which I do not notice a sun. In "light only," as I define it, the complete visual field, even as I look around (scan the visual surface), remains bright enough to be called light. There may be touches of other colors, or the brightness may not be of uniform intensity or of uniform whiteness, especially if I am tossing about. A blank visual field is not enough.

Either there is some form of a sun within the visual field or it looks like there is a sun or source of light out of sight. One sun or more and sometimes rays are the only forms that may appear in the field of light. This category, then, includes many experiences of a sun as a part of an ordinary or lucid dream and most of those in which the sun is a stable intense light.

I feel that "light only" is important as a category because it signals a release from ordinary visual dream imagery, while maintaining an intensification of visual experience. Darkness or a blank visual field also indicates a release from visual dream imagery. However, darkness, including my own creation of darkness by closing my eyes, never feels as important, exciting, or encouraging as a field of light. Darkness has never been numinous.

46. Stable Light, Spinning Head

A dream of mine demonstrates the location of a stable intense light outside the perceptual visual field, its fixed location within the scannable visual surface, and the persistence of the light through my waking up. The stable intense light in this case (April 1, 1982) was also the fullness of light.

> I was visiting friends and saw water pouring into the hall-way from the top of a huge tank. I ran to tell the hostess, and she proceeded to turn it off out of view. I walked back toward the door to the room that I had seen. I saw in the doorway from a distance three statues side by side at the right end of the room. People were at the other end of the room, the left end, but I could not see them.
>
> When I entered the room, the statues and the people were gone. I realized I was dreaming and, seeing the huge smooth wooden floor, I began to dance by spinning around. Then I saw a light like the sun at the upper edge of my

vision [a peripheral light]. Soon there was intense, vibrant light throughout the room, and thus throughout the visual field, and intense light was all I saw. The sun itself within the light remained above me.

I whirled around in the center of the room waving my arms. I imagined spinning at infinite speed, although I realized that my speed never really approached being infinite. My speed seemed to have a specific limit where it stayed. In spite of my spinning rapidly, the image of the sun itself remained at a fixed location as though above my head to the upper left. It continued to appear as being in a constant spot in relation to my head. When I turned my eyes upward somewhat to the left, I looked at it more directly. I woke up feeling queasy and with a quickened heartbeat.

Surprisingly, when I woke up with my eyes still shut, the image of the sun remained fixed in location as though some distance above my left eye, that is, outside of the perceptual visual field, even though the brightness over the rest of the visual field had faded away. The sun remained in a spatial relationship to my scanning eye just as it had while I was dreaming. It had now become hypnopompic imagery. While I kept my eyes shut, I could still turn my eyes up to the left to look at the sun more directly or turn my eyes away to see it indirectly, just as I had during the dream. The sun faded away gradually.

Since I woke up with the left side of my head inside my pillow, the light could not have originated outside my eye. Nor was it due to pressure of the pillow against my eye, for then the image would have been a pressed-eye image. It would have remained tied to my eye movement instead of being scannable.

The only break upon waking up came with the change from feeling my body dancing to feeling my body lying in bed. I was aware of the whole transition. From dreaming to lying awake, there had been continuity of visual field, light image, seeing, and scanning, demonstrating again that the one visual field continued from dreaming to lying awake. Normally, in ordinary dreaming and in lucid dreaming I am not aware of any continuity from dreaming to waking up. Only rarely have I been aware of it.

Evidently while I was dreaming and dancing, the visual field of both dream imagery and then of light was not off somewhere in a dream body of mine that was spinning around in a dream room. The location of the light that I saw remained anchored to my head, that is, the head of my sleeping body which became the head of my body awake, not in a dancing head. I saw all visual imagery of any kind within my physical body, not in a dancing dream head—just where I see my visual image when I am awake with my eyes open.

As usual, I was not seeing with my sleeping eyes or with dreamed eyes. The image of the sun itself lay above the limits of the perceptual/dream visual field, which made it look like I saw the light above my head. The perceptual mindset made it seem that I was looking from the usual viewpoint in the center of the unprojected visual image. I was seeing, but I was not looking from anywhere. When I "looked up" to see the light more directly, I was just moving my eyes up, but the eyes were not doing the seeing. In the next section I'll work a little more on conveying this idea.

Although the religious feeling was present but less intense than usual, the religious symbolism of the experience and the intensity of the light, upon later reflection, encouraged me to consider this event to be a version of the fullness of light. The three statues at the end of the room made me think (after I woke up) of the Trinity. Then, as I entered the room, the three disappeared, and I felt the presence of God as I danced in the center of the room.

47. The Light Above My Head

In a number of cases of the fullness of light, the fullness was preceded by my seeing a light above my head, seeming to move from directly behind me and then down in front of me. In the section before this I described a light that I saw above my head as I danced. I am not talking about a light that I need to lean my head back in order to look up to see. This is a light that I see above my head while I look straight ahead in front of me. I feel the need to clarify how I see a light above my head.

In Figure 3, I compare seeing the elementary visual field with seeing perceptually. The line E1-A1-E1 represents a vertical cut through the diameter of the elementary visual field. The arc E1-A-E1 represents a vertical cut through the center of the hemispheric projection of the elementary image as I look to the left. Lines D-D1 represent the upper and lower limits of the perceptual image on the flat visual field (on the right) and as seen with the perceptual mindset (on the left). I can only estimate how high or low the perceptual visual field reaches within the elementary visual field, and that height and lower limit may vary with individuals.

The visual image always makes my viewpoint to be located at A1, the center of the visual field, and the object of my attention to be at the center of the receding hemisphere, at A. With elementary imagery, I can see the whole hemispheric image (E1-A-E1) from the viewpoint at A1. It is as though I have lines of sight reaching in every direction from my viewpoint, even though there are no lines of sight actually present in the act of seeing.

During perception, every part of the perceptual image implies different lines of sight from the viewpoint at A1. No line of sight appears to connect A1 to anywhere between D and E1, because that would locate the visual object outside of the perceptual visual field (D-A-D). A visual object located between D and E1, for example, will lie where, thinking perceptually, I should not be able to see anything. It is always possible that I might not notice an image beyond the perceptual visual field, if there happened to be one, because anywhere outside the perceptual visual field lies very far from my focus of attention in the center of the visual field. It would take something very bright to be noticed that far from where my attention is directed. In fact, it is only in lucid dreams that I have occasionally noticed an intense light or anything else appearing outside of the perceptual visual field.

Let us suppose that during a lucid dream an intense light appears at the top of the elementary visual field at E1, which lies far outside of the perceptual visual field. I will probably not think at the time in terms of perceptual and elementary visual fields. I only know where the light is located and, because of my limited reasoning ability I might not make much of the fact that it lies at E1, directly above my viewpoint at A1, where I do not usually see anything.

Notice that the line of sight that seemingly sees the light (A1-E1) is straight up from my viewpoint, which acts as my dreamed eye. A line of sight that is straight up from my eye means that I seem to see straight up through and beyond my head. I see the light as located logically above my head. It does not look close enough to look like it is in my head. The line of sight forms a 90 degree angle with my central line of sight, the angle being A-A1-E1, while I am looking at A.

No matter what direction I look in within the visual surface, a light at the top of the elementary visual field will look like it is located above my head, because of that 90 degree angle. Of course, my head does not lie in the way of seeing the light. It is as though I see through my head, except that I am not dreaming my head, nor am I thinking about my head being in the way. This is the way that I see a light above my head in a lucid dream or how I might see the sun's first appearance above me during the fullness of light. To me it is just a fact that I can see in odd directions and I do not usually marvel at it at the time.

In the coming-of-the-sun part of the fullness, it was often as though I saw a sun move over my right eye as though from behind me. I began to see the light at E1, which lies above my head, and as it moved down the visual field (seen as moving down from E1to D or C and so on), it would seem to have come from behind me, passing over my head. In other cases, a light that I see at D1 in the figure, if I am awake, might appear to lie in the direction of my forehead at D, or in the direction of an eyebrow. If I am not awake, I might not be aware of my forehead or eyebrow. In the same manner, light that I see on the very left of the elementary visual field appears to be located in the left corner of my left eye.

It is usually difficult to judge someone else's description of subjective experiences of light. Nevertheless, I offer some possibilities as examples of other people seeing a light or other image where one cannot see perceptually.

This is from Augustine of Hippo:

> I entered into my inmost parts with you leading me on. I was able to do so because you had become my helper. I entered and saw with my soul's eye (such as it was) an unchanging Light above the same soul's eye, above my mind. It was not this common light that can be seen by all flesh, nor was it like a greater one of the same kind, as if this light should gleam forth more and more brightly and fill up everything with its greatness. (B. McGinn, 2006, p. 317)

It sounds like Augustine saw a great light that looked as though it was above his mind, that is, it looked as though it was above the level of his physical eyes, perhaps within the upper part of the elementary visual field, say at point C, D, or higher in Figure 3. Either that or he understood that it was above his soul's eye, or above his viewpoint (at A1). In any case, it seemed to be located above his mind.

So also Hildegard of Bingen:

And it came to pass in the eleven hundred and forty-first year of the incarnation of Jesus Christ, Son of God, when I was forty-two years and seven months old, that the heavens were opened and a blinding light of exceptional brilliance flowed through my entire brain. (S. Flanagan, 1998, p. 4)

To see a light fill one's brain seems to be to see it fill whatever lies within the head above the eyebrows, perhaps from E1 to D1 or C1 in Figure 3. Or it could even have filled the elementary visual field.

Swami Sivananda, in speaking about Hindu meditation, says:

For those who concentrate on the Trikuti, the space between the two eyebrows, the light appears in the forehead in the Trikuti, while for others who concentrate on the top of the head, Sahasrara Chakra, the light manifests on the top of the head. (Sivananda, 1975, p. 341)

For such people as he describes, the light might be seen at D1 (or higher) in Figure 3 and be understood to be seen at D, in the direction of his forehead or higher, above the perceptual visual field. The light at the top of the head would be at E1 and be seen as being in that direction because the angle of the line of sight would be at 90° compared to the central line of sight.

Elsewhere, Gopi Krishna (1970) describes in the context of Kundalini yoga an illumination that grew brighter and brighter at the top of his head, which would be at the top of the elementary visual field, at E1 in Figure 3.

I have no intention of trying to fit my personal observations into the scheme of the Hindu or tantric forms of yoga, but rather to point out how one can see light that seems to be upon the forehead or above the head. The Hindu religious or philosophical contexts that I have mentioned are different from mine, but I suggest that light is light and the phenomenon of how light is seen and how it is seen to lie in specific, even unusual, directions has some universal explanation, which does not depend on one's understanding of religion or philosophy.

Apparently lights and a variety of other elementary imagery have also appeared outside of the perceptual visual field in situations other than religious. Charles Tart (1969) reports that in a case of hypnosis a subject felt that she had light coming out from under her eyebrows. Richard Cytowic (1993) reports a woman who, in a case of synesthesia, felt that the space above her eyes was like a big screen, where she saw triangles, lines, and angles. Oliver Sacks reports cases of visual migraine aura in which patients see a "sort of angled crown or rainbow above the eyes" (Sacks, 1992, p. 66). Sacks also reports a case of "bereavement hallucination" in which the experiencer

> could see the face of Brooks [the deceased], larger than life, smiling, and very distinct, yet looking as if it were made of dewy gossamer. When he looked down, the vision disappeared, but for ten days he could see it a little above his head to the left. (Sacks, 2012, pp. 232–233)

The difference in the last case is that the hallucination was not of geometrical imagery or light, but a face located high within the elementary visual field, seemingly fixed in location above his head, so that, by scanning down, he could leave the image behind as an image to come back to.

Since an intense light appearing at the top of the elementary visual field would appear to be located above the head, it is reasonable to expect that lights or imagery of any sort that may be located at the lowest part of the elementary visual field might be seen as located far below the viewpoint and below the perceptual visual field. This light would be understood to lie in a direction directly down from the eye, in fact, lying within the lower body.

If we look at Gopi Krishna's account of the varieties of light that he has seen in the context of Kundalini yoga, we do find him seeing light in the lower part of his body. For example:

> But in my case there was one particular and unmistakable deviation from the usual type of vision: the most extraordinary sensation at the base of the spine followed by the flow of a radiant current through the spinal column to the head. (Krishna, 1970, p. 60)

Also:

> A silvery streak passed zigzag through the spinal cord, exactly like the sinuous movement of a white serpent in rapid flight. (*ibid.*, p. 66)

> At times, turning my attention upon myself, I distinctly saw my body as a column of living fire from the tips of my toes to the head in which numerous currents circled and eddied, causing at places whirlpools and vortices, all forming part of a vast heaving sea of light, perpetually in motion. It was not a hallucination, as the experience was repeated innumerable times. (*ibid.*, p. 91)

48. Fire

I have described the light of the fullness as intense, vibrant, and having a boiling effect. It looks active and alive just as the perceptual sun does, rather than calm like the perceptual moon or the disk-of-light version of stable intense lights. In the fullness of light, I know that I am not awake, and at times remember that this is the light in which I know the presence of God, and I have never thought that I was seeing fire during the fullness. Nevertheless, for some people, when they see, while awake, the intense, vibrant light that sometimes accompanies religious experience, they believe the light to be fire, at least at first.

Naturally, if the one seeing the light is awake or has been perceiving the surrounding world when the vision happens, the light appears to be from out there in the world. However, all seeing happens inwardly, whether it is a perceptual image or whether the image originates through internal processes or other causes. In any case, the fire is seen as something apart from oneself. Some examples of the light understood as fire follow.

This is the beginning of Richard Bucke's experience of light:

> They parted at midnight, and he had a long drive in a hansom (it was in an English city). His mind, deeply under the influence of the ideas, images and emotions called up by the reading and talk of the evening, was calm and peaceful. He was in a state of quiet, almost passive enjoyment. All at once, without warning of any kind, he found himself wrapped around as it were by a flame-colored cloud. For an instant he thought of fire, some sudden conflagration in the great city; the next, he knew that the light was within himself. Directly afterwards came upon him a sense of exultation, of immense joyousness accompanied or immediately followed by an intellectual illumination quite impossible to describe. (Bucke, 1923, pp. 9–10)

Next is the experience of light of a famous Indian convert to Christianity, Sadhu Sundar Singh. The experience began like this:

> He prayed and prayed without stopping; He besought God earnestly to deliver him from this uncertainty and unrest, and to give him peace; but there was no answer. He would not be discouraged, however, and continued to strive with God in prayer in the hope of finding peace.

Suddenly — towards half-past four — a great light shone in his little room. He thought the house was on fire, opened the door and looked out; there was no fire there. He closed the door and went on praying. Then there dawned upon him a wonderful vision: in the centre of a luminous cloud he saw the face of a Man, radiant with love. At first he thought it was Buddha or Krishna, or some other divinity, and he was about to prostrate himself in worship. Just then, to his great astonishment, he heard these words in Hindustani … ("Why do you persecute Me? Remember that I gave My life for you upon the Cross"). Utterly at a loss, he was speechless with astonishment. Then he noticed the scars of Jesus of Nazareth, whom until that moment he had regarded merely as a great man who had lived and died long ago in Palestine, the same Jesus whom he had so passionately hated a few days before. … In an instant he felt that his whole being was completely changed; Christ flooded his nature with Divine life; peace and joy filled his soul, and "brought heaven into his heart." (Heiler, 1970, pp. 35–36)

The last story of the coming of light is the experience of Moses at the burning bush. The story begins like this:

Moses was keeping the flock of his father-in-law Jethro, the priest of Midian; he led his flock beyond the wilderness, and came to Horeb, the mountain of God. There the angel of the Lord appeared to him in a flame of fire out of a bush; he looked, and the bush was blazing, yet it was not consumed. Then Moses said, "I must turn aside and look at this great sight, and see why the bush is not burned up." When the Lord saw that he had turned aside to see, God called to him out of the bush, "Moses, Moses!" And he said, "Here I am." … (Exodus 3:1–4)

Knowing that all perception as well as all other seeing happens internally, I hope I do justice to the story of Moses and the burning bush. The image of "fire" was internal as also the perceptual image of the bush, but the bush itself was outside in front of him. The bush would not burn up, because the seeing of "fire" was only internal and not caused by flames in the bush. The fire would be the intense vibrant light that sometimes accompanies an awareness of the presence of God.

49. Unapproachable Light

The apostle Paul, when writing to Timothy, spoke of God, "It is he alone who has immortality and dwells in unapproachable light, whom no one has ever seen or can see; to him be honor and eternal dominion. Amen" (I Tim. 6:16). I understand Paul to be referring to an experience of his own of the presence of God, apart from his vision of Christ on the Damascus road. But what does this mean, this grand picture of God dwelling in light? How can we understand it?

Paul in his day and even people today would think of light with the common understanding of light. That is, that light is some three-dimensional stuff that fills the sky above us or fills the room or the part of the room where I am reading under the lamp. That is the way we talk of light, and it is natural to think that way. I can see to read when I am in light, and I cannot read in darkness. If we think of God dwelling in light in this literal way, then we have God being present within this stuff called light. It is roughly the way I thought of God and light during the "Amazing Grace" and other experiences of the fullness of light.

An alternative to this way of thinking is that this whole picture of God dwelling in light is a metaphor. God is surrounded by light, meaning goodness, purity, truth, or something else positive. Even then, the metaphor of light is based upon light as a three-dimensional presence that fills space. Most people, even with our present scientific understanding, seem not to think about light waves or how the brain creates in us a subjective experience of brightness and seeing. Light seems to be stuff out there.

Paul would think of light as filling some space before the eyes (either the eyes that have retinas or the "eyes of the spirit," so to speak). What Paul appears to express in his letter to Timothy is his personal experience, once or perhaps more times, of the presence of God. He speaks of an intense brightness that accompanies his awareness of the presence of God. Rightly or wrongly, based on this verse, I like to think that I understand Paul's experience.

For me, the experiences of God's presence that I had while asleep were exactly as if God were present with me in the midst of the light that I saw. I knew at the time that God was not the light itself that I saw, but I felt that God was present there within the most intense brightness that I have ever seen. At the time of seeing light, I did not think of God as being inside me. I did not literally experience light in my retinas, for my eyes were shut in sleep. I did literally experience the brightness, which, like dreams, was not dependent on light waves reaching my eyes, but somehow seemed to be intimately associated with the presence of God.

Symeon the New Theologian describes his experience:

So I entered the place where I usually prayed and, mindful of the words of the holy man [that he had just talked to] I began to say, "Holy God." At once I was so greatly moved to tears and loving desire for God that I would be unable to describe in words the joy and delight I then felt. I fell prostrate on the ground, and at once I saw, and behold, a great light was immaterially shining on me and seized hold of my whole mind and soul, so that I was struck with amazement at the unexpected marvel and I was, as it were, in ecstasy. Moreover I forgot the place where I stood, who I was, and where, and could only cry out, "Lord, have mercy," so that when I came to myself I discovered that I was reciting this. (Symeon, 1980, p. 200)

Teresa of Avila also tells about the dwelling places within her interior castle and about the King who dwells in its center, where the light is. The gate of entry into this castle, which is our soul, is prayer and reflection. She says,

> It should be kept in mind here that the fount, the shining sun that is in the center of the soul, does not lose its beauty and splendor; it is always present in the soul, and nothing can take away its loveliness. (1979, p. 40)

> [T]urn your eyes toward the center, which is the room or royal chamber where the King stays. ... [S]urrounding this center room are many other rooms. ... [T]he sun that is in this royal chamber shines in all parts. (*ibid.*, p. 42)

I understand the light for Paul, Symeon, and Teresa to be literal experiences of intense brightness. And, as in my experience, the light is other than God. It is my own visual field lighting up with my awareness of God's presence.

50. Disappearing into Light

Just as, while dreaming, I can disappear into darkness, as I did at the school at the top of the hill (section 9), I may also disappear, that is, lose body awareness, during the fullness of light. When I direct my attention to the light and God, awareness of my body gradually decreases, sometimes to the point of disappearing. I believe that in this experience of October 18, 1982, I also lost body awareness in the fullness of light:

> I was at a wild party in Moorestown. I seemed to be the only one not drunk, and I left for home. I couldn't see my way very well because it was dark outside. I realized I was

dreaming, but I did not think at first of anything to do. I soon remembered to look off into space [in part, a memory of trying to eliminate dream imagery], but didn't remember God or the light or to concentrate on the darkness. I began to bob up and down. I soon remembered the possibility of seeing light, but could not think of what to do about it. I thought I saw a light briefly. Then I wasn't sure.

Then I did see a bright sun move from over my right eye as though from behind me. Next the sun appeared down in front of me. Its orb was not as large as usual, giving the effect of being a little more distant than usual. But the surrounding brightness filled my visual field. I was happy to see it, but I still could not think much. I had a feeling of the divine presence, but I did not experience as extreme joy and devotion as I have at other times. My feeling as well as my mental ability was subdued. I remembered my intention to shut my eyes to see whether the light would disappear by my doing so.

Since I tend to automatically do without discernment what I remember to do, I slowly shut my (dreamed?) eyes and opened them and shut them again. And then repeatedly shut and opened them rapidly. The light remained steady throughout as I saw my (probably dreamed) eyelids go up and down as though in front of the light.

Then I no longer felt any body movement and was aware only of the area around my eyes, which means only that I was aware of seeing. Although my mind was largely blank, I felt happy, quiet, and devotional. The last trace of dreaming (the body imagery) had disappeared. I was aware only of light and of God.

Shutting my eyes and continuing to see the light of the fullness is not really a paradox as I know now. I could shut my eyes, see my eyelids flutter, and then feel them stay shut, because presumably everything related to the shutting and fluttering of my eyelids was dreamed, and the light, as I mentioned before, was not dream imagery.

51. The Light of the Fullness

When I see the light of the fullness, the brightness covering the visual field is as intense and vibrant as the light next to the perceptual sun high in the sky on a clear day. I say "next to the sun" because when I look directly toward the perceptual sun at its most intense, I see the form of the sun itself as dark, with intense vibrant light surrounding the perceptual sun on all sides. The elementary visual field, except perhaps at times within the sun image itself, is usually the fullest intensification of a sun-like vibrant white, which has in it all the colors.

In the light's boiling effect, I have discerned tiny momentary appearances of individual colors. These minute appearances of color other than white look like they might be specks or tiny oscillating lines of light. In any case, they appear and leave so quickly, taking only a fraction of a second, that there is no time to examine them closely. I would guess that every tiniest element of light is one momentary appearance followed by another, as in a crowd of oscillating lines, and that constant activity would create the vibrancy. It is the appearance of these colors other than white that make it seem appropriate to call the light "all-color white."

The sun image itself within the fullness has greater variety from one experience to the next than does the rest of the field of light, although the sun is never dark. The sun varies from experience to experience in size, look, and location within the visual surface, except that I have never noticed it within the lower part of the visual field. In my first experience, although I saw an intensely bright peripheral light off to my left at first, when the whole visual field became bright, I did not notice a sun image. However, a sun was visible in all the other experiences of the fullness.

The sun's circumference is sometimes well-defined and sometimes it looks blurred. Once only, the sun's image was orange, bright, and huge enough to almost cover the visual field. There have been no multiple suns within the fullness, although there have been in other experiences. Sometimes suns on other occasions have had rays, but only in the "near-death" experience did the sun of the fullness have rays. Those rays were not arranged symmetrically around the sun.

Because I have a perceptual mindset during the fullness of light, I see the light as lying three-dimensionally in all directions around my viewpoint. I see it reaching beyond the limits of the perceptual visual field. It is also as though my head does not limit my view, although during the experience I accept things as they appear to be. The kinds of analyses and conclusions that I make with my lattice imagery are never remembered during the time of the fullness. When I wake up, I normally remember clearly whatever I saw and analyze it while awake.

My analysis has led me to understand that light does not emanate from God or from above or from anywhere outside the visual field. It is not a cloud of light, although because it appears to surround me it looks like it could be. It is not a simulation of light or a dream of light. It is an intensification of image itself, the "stuff" of visual dream imagery, hypnopompic imagery, and perception. The light does not disturb the eyes; the eyes are not involved with seeing the light of the fullness.

I need no spiritual or dream eyes in order to see the light of the fullness. Like all visual imagery, I see the visual field of light face-on at every point. However, because I do see light and whatever else there is to see, I feel at the time that I have eyes that do the seeing. Even as my body imagery disappears, I continue to see the light. The diminishment or disappearance of dreamed body awareness does not affect or stop my seeing of the light, because no eyes disappear with the loss of body imagery. No eyes were ever there. The light covering the visual field, like all other seeing, is spatially related to my body awareness as a whole and happens within my sleeping body.

It is within my own body that I become aware of the presence of God. As the Apostle Paul wrote, "[D]o you not know that your body is a temple of the Holy Spirit within you, which you have from God, and that you are not your own?" (I Cor. 6:19). I find God's presence with me, within this temple, which is my body.

It was impossible for me to imagine, desire, or anticipate such an experience of light so as to prepare me for seeing what I saw. I say this in light of the ongoing discussion about the nature of mystical experiences, in which Steven T. Katz says:

> [W]e must recognize that a right understanding of mysticism is not just a question of studying the reports of the mystic after the experiential event but also of acknowledging that the experience itself, as well as the form in which it is reported, is shaped by concepts which the mystic brings to, and which shape, his experience. (Katz, 1983, p. 4)

I do not want to get into the intricacies of this discussion, but only to make the comment that my reading about Moses and the burning bush, Saul's experience of the risen Christ on the road to Damascus, and the experience of Peter, James, and John on the mountain at the transfiguration, as well as my reading of Arjuna's vision of Vishnu in his supreme form, did not prepare me for the experience of the fullness of light. I was barely acquainted with the Christian mystics before I began to see light. Apart from the mystical events in the Bible and my teaching about Hinduism, the discussion of mysticism and religious experiences of light was essentially foreign to me before this journey — including in seminary.

When I was experimenting with dreamless sleep, I was not trying to have a religious experience of light nor did I think that I might. I could in no way anticipate an intensity and vibrancy of light so far surpassing what the eyes permit me to see during waking perception. Nor could I be prepared for light that reached far beyond the perceptual visual field in every direction. Nor could I imagine losing the awareness of my body as I watched the light. I had no idea of such experiences and did not know that they could happen in one's sleep.

Apparently an experience of the presence of God can take a variety of forms, and does not necessarily include light. Although the literal presence of overwhelming light is important to my experiences as it is for many others (see Dyczkowski, 1987; Eliade, 1965; Fedotov, 1948; Hollenback, 1996; Kapstein, 2004a, 2004b; Pulver, 1960; Symeon the New Theologian, 1980), the experience of the presence of God may not include light. Ignatius of Loyola, the founder of the Jesuits, experienced the presence of God without a vision of light as he sat lost in devotions beside the River Cardoner. Teresa of Avila often records knowing the presence of God without mentioning light.

For me, the fullness of light and knowledge of the presence of God appear to be intimately connected, although I do not confuse the light with God. Actually, one can read a lot of words from particular mystics who are fond of the word "light" and not know whether their word "light" is intended in any literal sense. However, in my reading, it is clear to me that many mystics of various religious backgrounds literally see light in their religious experience.

VI

The Presence of God

52. Finding God

The apostle Paul told the people of Athens:

> The God who made the world and everything in it, he who is Lord of heaven and earth, does not live in shrines made by human hands, nor is he served by human hands, as though he needed anything, since he himself gives to all mortals life and breath and all things. From one ancestor he made all nations to inhabit the whole earth, and he allotted the times of their existence and the boundaries of the places where they would live, so that they would search for God and perhaps grope for him and find him—though indeed he is not far from each one of us. (Acts 17:24–27)

In ancient India, there were seers who practiced meditation and searched for truth within their experience. In the *Śvetāśvatara Upaniṣad* 3:8, the seer declares, "I know that great person, having an appearance like the sun, beyond the darkness. Only by knowing him does one go beyond death. There is no other path to go on." I believe that the seer who composed these lines hundreds of years before the birth of Christ searched within himself and found God to be present with him within the experience of light.

Some Indian seers searched and found God. Some looked for the impersonal *brahman* which they believed underlies all existence. In Hinduism, both concepts, God and *brahman*, were developed, as well as countless other subtleties of thought about what is ultimately real. Sometimes, perhaps, one finds the ultimate that one searches for. Sometimes, what one finds does not depend on one's beliefs, goals, or practices at all. I was not searching for God or light, at least not consciously, when I began to experience the fullness of light. I was searching for dreamless sleep, whatever that was to be.

53. Knowing the Presence of God

When I am awake, I know that God is present with me. I remember it is so, and I believe it. However, I do not know it the way I know it in the fullness of light. In the fullness of light my knowledge of the presence of God is an unanalyzed, unquestioned, involuntary certainty about that moment, not a reasoning, a remembering, or a reaction to what I see and feel. I am aware of God. I know that God is present with me just as I know now that I am in my house writing this. The only difference may be that I do not feel the presence of my house, while I do feel the presence of God. It is an awareness of holiness. Any waking analysis on whether I had been right or wrong to believe that does not change that experience of knowing.

In the fullness of light, I feel that God is present to me in particular and that God is located near me. I am alone with God. I do not think of God as having a body or as being located in a specific direction. However, I feel that God is present in the light that I see everywhere around me. As I reflect on this while awake, I do not think of God as having come to be present with me, for God is always within me. But while going within myself, so to speak, by going to sleep and then somehow gradually losing contact with the dream, I have come to know God's presence. Not that my going deeply within myself is enough to bring about an experience of God, for being aware of the presence of God in this way is not something that I can make happen. To know God's presence is to experience grace.

Whatever else I think or do during the fullness, my over-riding thought and emotion center on God. The intense joy and compulsion to worship that accompany that knowledge are largely involuntary. My joy, devotional feelings, and under-standing that God is present happen to me as one indivisible piece. It feels like joy and devotional feelings are not reactions to the presence, but part of the presence. I think of the whole combination as "knowing the presence of God." Joy and devotional feelings are emotions closely associated with love. To enjoy and to revere God are the two sides of that love, even though I have not used the word "love" when recording my experiences.

To know the presence of God is, for me, to experience numinosity. "Numinosity" means to me an overwhelming non-rational awareness of the presence of what is holy. By "numinosity" I mean largely, though not precisely, as it is so thoroughly discussed by Rudolph Otto (1958). I am not aware first of the presence of God (of the numinous) and then react with feelings of numinosity. My feelings are given to me.

In discussions of numinosity, I read that it may include awe, humility, fear, fascination, or urgency. The feeling of numi-nosity need not be the same for all people. Neither humility nor fear crosses my mind during the fullness. I feel neither rebuked nor afraid. My joy in the presence of God appears to preclude fear or dread and must surpass any emotion that I have known while awake.

I want to comment on Ninian Smart's (1996) presentation of numinosity as an apprehension of a fearful outside Other, who is "to be shuddered at" (p. 167), an experience that is to be contrasted with the experience of nonduality, which he says is supremely serene. It is possible to be overcome with numinous feelings, which I claim and which I associate mainly with an awareness of holiness, without shuddering at God's presence. And I am not sure how to understand his "outside Other," unless "outside" means no more than the otherness of God. It is hard to think of God as outside, when I find God by becoming totally unaware of the world outside me and of my sleeping body. My experience of the presence of God happens totally within me.

My feelings impel me to worship. I praise God, sing, or repeat scripture verses, aloud or silently. I have little self-control. It is not that I am impelled to repeat specific words or to sing rather than to pray. I am impelled to devotional action, while retaining some apparent freedom to select from my limited memory what to say or do. Or, probably, I do not select, but say what comes to mind.

Scripture says, "No one has ever seen God" (John 1:18). In the fullness of light, I do not see God. But as I understand what happens, I "perceive" God through my awareness of God's presence in me and the intense devotional feelings that come upon me. So that, just as I visually perceive the world when I am awake by experiencing my visual perceptual image, I perceive God's presence also through experiencing my awareness of the presence and holiness of God, my urge to worship, and my joy. I am what I feel. I am my perception of God. Knowing God's presence in this manner becomes a part of me, at least for a while. I hope I am not carrying this analysis too far, but these thoughts have been helpful to me as I try to understand the experience of the fullness of light as authentic religious experience, metaphor, and as a perception of God.

54. The Trinity

Some writers believe that mystical experience is necessarily shaped by the concepts that the mystic takes to the experience (for example, Katz, 1978). A Hindu has a Hindu experience, they suggest, and a Christian has a Christian experience. A

Christian mystic is likely to encounter Jesus, the Trinity, or a personal God. Although I am a Christian and Christ is my light, I am not sure how to think of my experience of the fullness of light in terms of the Trinity or how to find Christ as a distinct part of my experience. This has not been a concern for me, but it has been a puzzle.

God is the essential part of the experience. I am aware of God. I worship God spontaneously, and my joy is in God. It is the Holy Spirit who brings me to call out "God is love" or "Blessed is the name of the Lord," when I experience the light. In the most intense experiences, my calling these verses is beyond my control. I find meaning in Paul's letter to the Romans (8:15–16), where he writes, "When we cry, 'Abba! Father!' it is that very Spirit bearing witness with our spirit that we are children of God." The Spirit of God moves me to shout or simply to repeat these praises from my limited memory. I find that I have spontaneously called God "Father" during four occasions of the fullness of light.

While awake, I have tended to think of God as spirit, neither male nor female and I have tried to refer to God accordingly. Yet my spontaneously calling "Father" during the fullness of light makes that name for God special for me. I never thought ahead that I would call God "Father." I called out what came to me.

I feel that the temptation here is to make too much of a distinction between God and the Spirit of God, and this leads to over-analyzing. As for Christ, I am his. He is my way, my truth, and my life, and he has taken me into the realm of God. I do not doubt that Christ, "the true light that enlightens everyone coming into the world" (John 1:9), is in the experience.

In the fullness of light, the Trinity has not divided into three for me to see the part that each one plays in the experience. The Trinity is an important theological concept and an official doctrine of the church since the year 325 CE. However, I see in Scripture not only the reasoning behind the distinctions made among the Trinity in theological doctrine, but a blurring of the distinctions.

If we look at the fourteenth chapter of the Gospel of John, we find Jesus meeting with his disciples in the upper room shortly before he was crucified. He tells them that the Spirit of truth, the Holy Spirit, will be in them (14:17). At the same time, he explains that he, Christ, will also be in them. He says, "I am in my Father, and you in me, and I in you" (14:20). He adds, "Those who love me will keep my word, and my Father will love them, and we will come to them and make our home with them" (14:23). That is, Christ and God the Father will be with them.

God, the Word of God, the Spirit of God, is the one who lives in me, and I believe that to pick the Trinity apart in analyzing my experience is to fuss too much.

55. Absorption

In the literature on mysticism, there is discussion of the experience of absorption into or merger with some transcendent reality, be it God, *brahman*, or otherwise. In Pike's study of Christian mysticism, he describes absorption in this way: "Here, it is not just that contact has been made. God has come to *contain* the soul: the soul is immersed in and absorbed by God—that is, submerged in or enwrapped by him" (1992, p. 8).

I find that John of the Cross speaks of absorption in two ways. Writing in his first redaction of *Living Flame of Love*, he says that God

> absorbs the soul, above all being, in the Being of God, for He has encountered it and pierced it to the quick in the Holy Spirit, Whose communications are impetuous when they are full of fervor, as is this communication. (1926, p. 56)

Here the experience of absorption is spoken of as being into God.

At another place of the text, the experience of John of the Cross is spoken of as being absorbed into light.

> In this state, the soul is like the crystal that is clear and pure; the more degrees of light it receives, the greater concentration of light there is in it, and this enlightenment continues to such a degree that at last it attains a point at which the light is centred in it with such copiousness that it comes to appear to be wholly light, and cannot be distinguished from the light, for it is enlightened to the greatest possible extent and thus appears to be light itself. (*ibid.*, p. 41)

Perhaps no literal light is intended at all in this passage, but I read it as very possibly a description of an occasion of intense light in which nothing is left of the body imagery of the experiencer. He indeed appears to have been overwhelmed by light as he gives attention to the presence of God in light.

It seems to me that absorption, as an experience, depends largely on the disappearance of one's body imagery while retaining the visual, felt, or assumed presence of some powerful other to be absorbed into. There may be other experiences that can give one the sense of absorption, but the loss of body imagery, which would need to be dreamed body imagery, is the key factor, as far as I can see. I cannot think of what the absorption of my soul in God would be like, in part because I do not know how to think about my soul. Of course, I have a lot to learn. However, this is what I am thinking now.

I don't find that disappearing or absorption is something that I can particularly think about while it is happening, because the loss of body imagery depends upon a minimum of thinking about my (dreamed) body or about myself during the experience. However, the details of a possible absorption, if any, should be recallable upon waking reflection.

For the record, I never interpreted my experiences, either during a disappearance into darkness or into light, as a literal absorption into anything. If I had not had a history of unusual dream experiences and had not repeatedly analyzed my experiences of darkness and light critically, I might have concluded at some time that I had been absorbed into God or at least into the light. With one caveat—that as long as I see either darkness or light, I have the impression that I still have eyes to see. My eyes have not disappeared into God or light, it would seem, because I am still seeing. That is at least what I might think. That I would not have eyes to see with because the image is itself the seeing is too sophisticated a thought to come easily to me during the fullness of light, even if I had thought about it while awake. My mind at the time is not so clear. So what I can talk about here is absorption as a possible under-standing of the loss of body awareness while knowing the presence of God.

My greatest experience of the elimination of body imagery in darkness was in the dream in which I climbed the hill and walked out to the end of the bamboo platform and closed my eyes in order to concentrate on the darkness and then on my imaginary flame (see section 9). One of the greatest losses of body imagery in light appears to be the time in which, as I gave my attention to the light, I could not think very well, and I tested my seeing of light while opening and shutting my (dreamed?) eyelids (see section 50).

I see important ways in which absorption in darkness differs from absorption in the fullness of light. I also see similarities. In the one, there is seeing only of darkness, and in the other, the seeing only of light. The disappearance of body imagery in the one case happens not too differently from its disappearance in the other. In both cases, I direct my attention upon what I see, and it is by my concentration or attention upon darkness, light, or God that my body imagery begins to dissipate. Because a comparison can be made, it would be good to note the differences between absorption into darkness and into light, when absorption is understood to be the disappearance of body awareness.

1. *Content of the experience.* In absorption in darkness, the content is only darkness. No intellectual or emotional content accompanies the disappearance of body imagery as I concentrate on the darkness. The experience has no clear meaning for me, either during the disappearance or upon waking reflection. There is little, if anything, to remember, and I believe that my interpretation of what happened would need to be thought about afterward.

Absorption into light, however, has intense positive content. There is light and I am aware of the presence of God. I feel devotional and am happy, usually intensely joyful, during the whole process. The light itself is an overwhelming presence in a way that darkness is not. The fullness is a deeply religious experience. I know the meaning of the event—that God is present—while it happens and my knowing does not depend on an interpretation afterwards.

2. *Awareness of another.* Unlike light, darkness is a passive presence and does not demand my attention. Concentrating my attention on the darkness is not very different from simply keeping my attention from wandering and keeping my eyes from moving while I see darkness. While it is happening, I do not think of darkness as being something other than myself. It is my darkness. It is not another. There is no other.

In the fullness of light, I am intensely aware of what I think is other than myself, in a way that I cannot be during darkness. Joy, reverence, and body imagery I know to be mine, but God and the light I understand at the time to be other than myself. During the experience, I do not realize that the intense light is a manifestation of my own visual processes and is in fact a manifestation of myself. It is the object of my seeing. My extreme joy, devotional impulses, and awareness of the presence of God all orient me toward God, whom I know to be other than me and who is of much more importance to me than is the light. Simply to be aware of the presence of God in the light is to be very aware of God as distinct from myself.

3. *Means of achieving.* I close my (dreamed) eyes in a dream and create darkness by my own efforts. I normally did this as I also intentionally tried to eliminate dream imagery. Since the appearance of darkness does not demand my attention the way light does, I must choose to keep my attention on the darkness. Absorption in darkness does not just happen to me. I willfully create the darkness by closing my eyes and willfully give my attention to it.

Even though I can willfully stop my activity, concentrate, and eliminate visual or body imagery while dreaming, nothing that I do has noticeably caused the fullness of light to happen. The experience of light and of the presence of God happens to me involuntarily and spontaneously, whether I have eliminated dream imagery or not. It is not my work. Theologically speaking, it is an act of grace. The presence of God demands my attention even more than does the light. As the light and the presence of God draw my attention away from my body, I lose body awareness without trying, and I disappear gradually into the light.

4. *My location within the original dream.* In my best case of elimination of body awareness during darkness, I was up in the high bamboo construction that I entered from the top of a hill. In this and in my two other best cases of elimination within darkness, I was high up on a hill when I became lucid, when I concentrated on the darkness, and when I lost my ground support.

In the dreams that led up to my thirteen experiences of the fullness of light, I never dreamed that I was up on a hill or upstairs. In fact, in spite of the common reference to mountaintop experiences, my progression to the fullness of light always began from dreams in which I was on ground level, either outside on the ground or inside a building on the ground floor. Sometimes I went from being on ground level to release from the ground to floating. When I float, it does not appear to mean that I am then above the ground. There is simply no longer any ground for me to be connected to or to float above. Floating then leads to a gradual loss of body imagery in the fullness of light.

In fact, in all 41 dreams that ended up with a visual field full of light only, whether it was the fullness of light or lesser forms of light only across the visual field, I became lucid only while on ground level or while already released from the ground or after falling and never in a dream in which I was up on a hill or upstairs. I did have significant dreams that took place up high, but they took a different turn. The next difference (number 5) does appear to help explain why there is a difference between a high and a low location in the dream.

5. *Mental ability.* Some argue that the dreamer must have the mental abilities of waking consciousness and be able to think clearly before a dream can be called lucid (for example, LaBerge, 1985; Tart, 1972, 1984; Tholey, 1988). However, I don't believe that in my 764 (at least) lucid dreams I have experienced anything close to my waking mental abilities. I remember very little about the world or even about events of my own life. I have never remembered where I was sleeping, in spite of trying. Nor do I ever think very clearly. And I am not aware of my limitations. I may do things that make no sense.

After six years of lucid dreaming, I made a study of my mental ability in lucid dreams for an article in *Lucidity Letter* (Gillespie, 1984). I considered myself to have greater mental ability in a lucid dream when I could remember what experiment I had planned to do, or, if not remembering it, I could think of a reasonable alternative experiment. I considered myself to have less mental ability if I did not remember that I had planned something to do in the dream, or remembered that I had planned something but could not think of what it was, or when trying to think of what I could do, I could not think of anything sensible.

I found that I had greater mental ability in 72% (34/47) of all lucid dreams, up to that point, where I was up on a hill or upstairs, with an 81% (22/27) success rate in dreams in which I was specifically upstairs. On the other hand, I had greater mental ability in only 50% (102/202) of all ground-level dreams and in any kind of dreams in which I was already floating or flying (14/28).

In fact, in statistics that covered all lucid dreams (282) through July, 1981, in only 15% (2/13) of dreams that led to the fullness of light did I remember enough of what I had planned to do to consider myself to be mentally successful. In addition, in only 15% (6/41) of all dreams that eventually became any version of what I call "light only" dreams, did I have greater mental ability.

Therefore, my eliminations of body awareness in darkness were achieved most easily in lucid dreams where I was up high in the dream and my mental ability was best. Recall that, in my dream with the greatest absorption in darkness, I not only went up the hill first and out onto a high platform (upstairs, so to speak), but there was a school at the top of the hill and students everywhere. In that dream I did, in fact, remember what I intended to do and carried it out. Besides my being up high, the school and the students perhaps represented my greater mental ability at that moment.

Generally speaking, my experiences of the fullness of light and absorption into the light have not developed within lucid dreams in which I had the greatest mental clarity, but in dreams in which I had the least. I felt the presence of God and saw the most intense light at the conclusion of lucid dreams where my mind was least mentally acute and least able to remember or reason—where there was the greatest forgetting.

56. Ineffability

William James described the first mark of mysticism as ineffability, meaning that no adequate report of its contents can be given in words (James, 1961). In fact, he said that incommunicableness is the keynote of all mysticism. Later scholars have repeated James on this matter. Denise L. and John T. Carmody suggest that with mysticism, "the very substance, the bare minimum necessary for speaking significantly at all [about it], cannot be captured adequately in human terms" (1996, p. 21). Charles Tart mentions that the ineffability of mysticism means that it is "beyond our ability to conceptualize" (1975, p. 51). Ninian Smart explains that "mystics refer to their experiences as ineffable, or at any rate to the 'object' of their experiences as ineffable," meaning, among other things, that they are "'indescribable', 'inexpressible', 'unspeakable', 'indefinable', 'unutterable', 'incomprehensible', and so on" (1978, p. 17).

In this account, I have tried to describe, express, define, conceptualize, and explain some confusing and overpowering events associated with my experiences of the presence of God in light. Therefore, I would like to say something about ineffability, within the bounds of my own experience. I begin with Matthew T. Kapstein's observation that "ineffability in truth marks nothing at all" (2004b, p. 269). I presume that he means that the word "ineffability," at least the way the word is used, tells us nothing about the experience itself, but only that the mystic cannot describe what happened. I believe that the word "ineffable" does tell us something, but not much. In fact, we do know something about the experiences of many mystics because they have said something about what happens, sometimes a lot. Their written accounts are available to us.

Although it is said that all mystical experience is ineffable and cannot be put into words, perhaps that is most true about what are said to be formless, contentless events, such as pure consciousness and other suggested examples discussed in

Forman (1990b). It seems to me that if an experience is content-less, there must be no content to remember or describe anyway. On that matter, I am willing to learn more, but that is how it looks to me now.

Not everything that happens in mysticism will be indescribable. For example, a visual field full of intense light, the disappearance of body imagery, the feeling of joy, or seeing a light above one's head can all be put into words, as I have done. The word "ineffable" is likely to correspond to some quality within mystical experience with content rather than experience without content. There may be feelings of numinosity, confusion, disorientation, or of being overwhelmed by light. The memories of these feelings or the feelings themselves may even stay with the mystic for some time afterward and remain difficult to put into words when the event is over.

Judging from my own experience, the foremost cause of ineffable feelings is awareness of the presence of God, of whom I am intensely aware. God lies beyond my introspection, as do all my unconscious processes, within which God works. God is neither seen nor heard, but I know God is there. The effect of God's presence with its feelings of numinosity, reverence, joy, and the compulsion to worship I can write about only within limits. The feeling has no parallel in other parts of my life and by itself would be enough to warrant the word "ineffable." In fact, the word "ineffable," as I see it, is probably *primarily* due to the knowledge of the presence of God, when there is such presence, or of the immensity of what is happening.

The presence of any light of size or intensity while asleep is impressive. When the light is bright like the full moon or more intense than the sun, it is beyond the normality of dreaming. The light of the fullness has been, for me, an essential part of knowing the presence of God. The intensity of the light has been greater than any experience of light that I have been able to bear while awake. Besides the intensity of the whole visual field of light, the location of the sun where I should not be able to see it increases its contribution to my disorientation. The lesser stable intense lights also are neither dream-like nor percept-like, and may be seen outside, even far outside, of the perceptual visual field and may easily contribute to ineffability. Even having my body seemingly being tossed around among the stars is rather startling.

Lucidity may also play a part in feelings of ineffability. Just knowing that one is not awake can feel strange or unfamiliar, especially for those not used to being lucid in sleep. Being lucid, I am more likely to notice some dream-type inconsistencies and discontinuities. When I talk about my lucidity, however, I must take into account how my lucid dreaming differs from others'. Deidre Barrett (1992) has found that the degree of lucidity in dreaming varies both in individuals and among individuals. Even though I sometimes become lucid enough to catch the anomalies of dreaming and thereafter to stay lucid, my memory and mental abilities seem to stay closer to ordinary dream level than to waking level.

Other contributions to ineffability are surely found in the way dream imagery and vision work. In the experience of the fullness of light, for me, the effect of dreaming carries over primarily in my body imagery. As I find myself surrounded by light, I am attracted to God and the light. As in dreams, my attention directed to one object helps to eliminate what I no longer attend to. As my attention is directed to God and the light, I lose awareness of standing on the ground and I float up, and gradually I lose body awareness until, as a body, I virtually disappear, except that I continue to see. None of this is like normal experience.

The element of how vision works that is most evident in contributing to ineffability is the contrast between seeing imagery within the perceptual visual field and seeing imagery beyond the limits of the perceptual visual field. I may see other forms of light or other imagery beyond the limits of the perceptual visual field, even in the corner of my eye, at the level of my forehead, even above the top of my head, or straight down seemingly from the location of my eye. This is how the seeing of elementary imagery, including certain lights, works. Such imagery is seen not only higher or lower than the perceptual visual field, but in a direction in which the line of sight is at a greater angle than usual in relation to the central line of sight. As an example, the line of sight to the light above my head passes through where my head should be. In the case of the fullness of light, much of the light lies in directions I should not be able to see anything. Even though this may not all be analyzed at the time, these unusual appearances will contribute to the feeling of unfamiliarity.

Any imagery that remains in a fixed location within the visual surface, such as stable intense lights, would be difficult to integrate with our perceptual mindset. Most evident to me has been the appearance of a sun in front of my face that remained scannable there in spite of my turning my head. Peripheral lights, by definition, lay beyond the perceptual visual field, but also remained in place so that I could always look toward them and away from them. I have no idea to what extent stable intense lights, especially the fullness of light, have played a part in other people's spiritual experience.

Even though I understand some causes of ineffability, I do not begin to understand the mystery of God and God's presence in me — how or even why the fullness of light happens, how God interacts with the body and the brain, and what, in fact, really happens beyond the details of what I experience. God is infinitely more complex than what my little bit of experience tells me. I have only begun to put into words what has happened. I must still stress that the greater part of ineffability, for me, is the numinosity, the joy and reverence that overcomes me through knowing the presence of God.

I have not included the seeing of geometrical imagery as taking part in mystical experience. However, what I say about mystical experiences probably overlaps with some experiences of hypnopompic or hallucinatory imagery, which may create ineffable feelings also.

Final Thoughts

As the Preacher said, for everything there is a season. The season for my lucid dreaming has finished. I recorded one in 2013 and, before that, one in 2010. The lucid dreams came on their own. Rarely, I went to bed preparing myself to recognize that I was dreaming, but I wouldn't know whether I really ever helped bring about my lucidity in dreams. Within that time, the season for my knowing the presence of God in light ran from 1981 into 1985. Again, I can't say that I ever played a part in bringing about the fullness of light, at least not that I know of. That season came only for a while through the grace of God.

Other experiences during those days also had their season. The time for my seeing what I called "light only" during my dreams lasted from 1981 through 1993. The disk of light I saw five times in the period from 1981 to 1983.

The hypnopompic lattice imagery was different from anything I have mentioned so far, because I was not asleep. Its season lasted from 1985 through 1990. The lattice season began when we moved into a new apartment, where light came through the casement windows behind the head of our bed. Even then, I had to remember to direct my attention to the darkness that I saw.

No experience of light or visual imagery that I have mentioned so far was something that I got good at and was able to keep going forever, because each was a gift. I didn't do it. Each gift had its time and then stopped. I thought of visual imagery as my specialty, and I took advantage of it and studied it, but I did not make it happen, that I know of.

More visual imagery has happened since then that did not become a part of the story I have told here. I have now had several years of seeing hypnopompic oscillating imagery, three types which I call rotating, centric, and vertical. They came without my help from 1990 through 1993. Someday, they will make another story. I began to see migraine auras in 2001, mostly all without the accompanying headaches. These are still in season up to the present (2018).

The religious experiences have been the focus of this manuscript. I regret that I have mostly analyzed and told of my experiences and don't feel that I have been able to show the way for others to approach the knowledge of God in this way. In my own way, I feel that I have been doing theology, the study of God. God is never before the microscope, but the personal experience of knowing the presence of God in this rare unasked-for manner can be studied. This, it seems, I was asked to do. What I found out about seeing and scanning comes with it, and I felt that all that was also my spiritual duty to share.

Some of the concepts about vision that I have shared make difficult reading, I know, and I've worked and worked to make all this clearer, and I'm afraid I was not always successful. Well, I have to stop some time before my own season here is over. I would like to think that somehow I have been a help to this world.

George Gillespie
September 15, 2018

References

Abhishiktananda (1974). *Guru and disciple.* London: S.P.C.K.

Abhishiktananda (1975). *The further shore.* Delhi: I.S.P.C.K.

Abhishiktananda (1976). *Hindu-Christian meeting point: Within the cave of the heart.* Delhi: I.S.P.C.K.

Arnheim, R. (1969). *Visual thinking.* Berkeley, CA: University of California Press.

Barrett, D. (1992). Just how lucid are lucid dreams? *Dreaming, 2,* pp. 221–228.

Bhagavad-Gītā.

Bhattacharya, B. (Ed.). (1967). *Guhyasamāja tantra or tathāgataguhyaka.* Baroda, India: Oriental Institute.

Bible, New Revised Standard Version.

Block, N. (1983). Mental pictures and cognitive science. *Philosophical Review, 92,* pp. 499–541.

Boyd, R.H.S. (1975). *An introduction to Indian Christian theology.* Madras, India: The Christian Literature Society.

Bṛhadāraṇyaka Upaniṣad.

Bryant, B. (1992). *The wheel of time sand mandala: Visual scripture of Tibetan Buddhism.* San Francisco, CA: HarperSanFrancisco.

Bucke, R.M. (1923). *Cosmic consciousness: A study in the evolution of the human mind.* New York: E.P. Dutton.

Carmody, D.L. & Carmody, J.T. (1996). *Mysticism: Holiness East and West.* New York: Oxford University Press.

Castaneda, C. (1972). *Journey to Ixtlan: The lessons of Don Juan.* Harmondsworth, UK: Penguin Books.

Cytowic, R.E. (1993). *The man who tasted shapes*. Cambridge, MA: MIT Press.

Dalai Lama (1990) *Freedom in exile: The autobiography of the Dalai Lama*. New York: HarperCollins.

Déchanet, J.-M. (1960). *Christian yoga*. New York: Perennial Library.

Dennett, D.C. (1991). *Consciousness explained*. Boston, MA: Little, Brown.

Dennett, D.C. (1992). The nature of images and the introspective trap. In B. Beakley & P. Ludlow (Eds.), *The philosophy of mind: Classical problems/contemporary issues* (pp. 211–216). Cambridge, MA: MIT Press.

De Valois, R.L. & De Valois, K.K. (1988) *Spatial vision*. New York: Oxford University Press.

Dowman, K. (1985). *Masters of Mahāmudrā: Songs and histories of the eighty-four Buddhist siddhas*. Albany, NY: State University of New York Press.

Dyczkowski, M.S.G. (1987). *The doctrine of vibration: An analysis of the doctrines and practices of Kashmir Shaivism*. Albany, NY: State University of New York Press.

Eliade, M. (1964). *Shamanism: Archaic techniques of ecstasy* (W.R. Trask, Trans.). Princeton, NJ: Princeton University Press. (Original work published 1951.)

Eliade, M. (1965) Experiences of the mystic light. In Eliade, M. (Ed.), *The two and the one* (J.M. Cohen, Trans., pp. 19–77). Chicago, IL: University of Chicago Press. (Original work published 1962.)

Eliade, M. (1969). *Yoga: Immortality and freedom* (W.R. Trask, Trans.). Princeton, NJ: Princeton University Press. (Original work published 1954.)

Encyclopaedia Britannica (fourteenth edition).

Evans-Wentz, W.Y. (Ed.). (1958). *Tibetan yoga and secret doctrines*. London: Oxford University Press.

Faraday, A. (1972). *Dream power*. London: Hodder and Stoughton.

Fedotov, G.P. (Ed.). (1948). *A treasury of Russian spirituality*. New York: Sheed & Ward.

Flanagan, S. (1998). *Hildegard of Bingen: A visionary life* (2nd ed.). London: Routledge.

Gackenbach, J.I. (1992–93). Adaptiveness of childhood transpersonal experiences in two Cree women: A study. *Lucidity, 11* (1 & 2), pp. 107–122.

Garfield, P. (1979). *Pathway to ecstasy: The way of the dream mandala.* New York: Holt, Rinehart and Winston.

Gibson, J.J. (1986). *The ecological approach to visual perception.* Hillsdale, NJ: Lawrence Erlbaum.

Gillespie, G. (1984). Statistical description of my lucid dreams. *Lucidity Letter, 3* (4), pp. 6–10.

Gillespie, G. (1988). Without a guru: An account of my lucid dreaming. In J.I. Gackenbach & S. LaBerge (Eds.), *Conscious mind, sleeping brain: Perspectives on lucid dreaming* (pp. 343–350). New York: Plenum.

Gillespie, G. (1990). Use of subjective information in scientific psychology: III. The internal image during visual perception: An introspectionist analysis. *Perceptual and Motor Skills, 70,* pp. 963–983.

Gillespie, G. (1992). Light in lucid dreams: A review. *Dreaming, 2,* pp. 167–179.

Gillespie, G. (2000). John Woolman's light in the night: An analysis. *Dreaming, 10,* pp. 149–160.

Gillespie, G. (2009). Stable intense lights: A distinct class of light imagery seen in lucid dreaming. *DreamTime, 26* (1), pp. 14–15.

Gillespie, G. (2014). A pilgrimage into dreamless sleep. In R. Hurd & K. Bulkeley (Eds.), *Lucid dreaming: New perspectives on consciousness in sleep* (Vol. 2, *Religion, creativity, and culture,* pp. 291–299). Santa Barbara, CA: Praeger.

Gillespie, G. (2017). Attention with a narrow focus. *Autonomy, The Critical Journal of Interdisciplinary Autism Studies, 1* (5). Retrieved from http://www.larry-arnold.net/Autonomy/index.php/autonomy/article/view/AR19/html.

Guenther, H.V. (Trans.). (1963). *The life and teaching of Nāropa.* Oxford: Oxford University Press.

Gyatso, G.K. (1982). *Clear light of bliss: Mahamudra in Vajrayana Buddhism*. London: Wisdom.

Haber, R.N. (1969, April). Eidetic images. *Scientific American, 220* (4), pp. 36–44.

Haber, R.N. (1979). Twenty years of haunting eidetic imagery: Where's the ghost? *The Behavioral and Brain Sciences, 2*, pp. 583–594.

Hartmann, E. (1975). Dreams and other hallucinations: An approach to the underlying mechanism. In R.K. Siegel & L.J. West (Eds.), *Hallucinations: Behavior, experience, and theory* (pp. 71–79). New York: Wiley.

Hartmann, E. (1998). *Dreams and nightmares: The origin and meaning of dreams*. Cambridge, MA: Perseus.

Heiler, F. (1970). *The gospel of Sadhu Sundar Singh* (Abridged, O. Wyon, Trans.). Lucknow, India: Lucknow Publishing House.

Heruka, T.N. (1982). *The life of Marpa the translator: Seeing accomplishes all* (Nālandā Translation Committee, Trans.). Boulder, CO: Prajñā Press.

Hollenback, J.B. (1996). *Mysticism: Experience, response, and empowerment*. University Park, PA: Pennsylvania State University Press.

Horowitz, M.J. (1975). Hallucinations: An information-processing approach. In R.K. Siegel & L.J. West (Eds.), *Hallucinations: Behavior, experience, and theory* (pp. 163–195). New York: Wiley.

Hubel, D.H. (1988). *Eye, brain, and vision*. New York: Scientific American Library.

Hume, R.E. (1949). *The thirteen principal Upanishads translated from the Sanskrit*. Madras, India: Oxford University Press.

Hunt, H.T. (1989). *The multiplicity of dreams*. New Haven, CT: Yale University Press.

Hunt, H.T. (1991). Lucid dreaming as a meditative state: Some evidence from long-term meditators in relation to the cognitive-psychological bases of transpersonal phenomena. In J. Gackenbach & A. Sheikh (Eds.), *Dream images: A call to mental arms* (pp. 265–285). Amityville, NY: Baywood.

Huxley, A. (1990). *The doors of perception* and *Heaven and Hell*. New York: Harper & Row.

James, W. (1918). *The principles of psychology* (Vols. 1–2). New York: Dover.

James, W. (1961). *The varieties of religious experience: A study in human nature*. New York: Macmillan.

John of the Cross (1962). *Living flame of love*. Garden City, NY: Doubleday, Image Books.

Johnston, W. (Ed.). (1973). *The cloud of unknowing and the book of privy counseling*. New York: Doubleday, Image Books.

Julesz, B. (1971). *Foundations of cyclopean perception*. Chicago, IL: University of Chicago Press.

Jung, C.G. (1968). The symbolism of the mandala. In *The collected works of C.G. Jung: Vol. 12. Psychology and alchemy* (R.F.C. Hull, Trans., 2nd ed., pp. 95–223). Princeton, NJ: Princeton University Press.

Jung, C.G. (1969a). Concerning mandala symbolism. In *The collected works of C.G. Jung: Vol. 9, 1. The archetypes and the collective unconscious* (R.F.C. Hull, Trans., 2nd ed., pp. 355–384). Princeton, NJ: Princeton University Press.

Jung, C.G. (1969b). Psychology and religion. In *The collected works of C.G. Jung: Vol. 11. Psychology and religion: West and East* (R.F.C. Hull, Trans., 2nd ed., pp. 3–105). Princeton, NJ: Princeton University Press.

Kapstein, M.T. (Ed.). (2004a). *The presence of light: Divine radiance and religious experience*. Chicago, IL: University of Chicago Press.

Kapstein, M.T. (2004b). Rethinking religious experience: Seeing the light in the history of religions. In Kapstein, M.T. (Ed.), *The presence of light: Divine radiance and religious experience* (pp. 265–299). Chicago, IL: University of Chicago Press.

Katz, S.T. (Ed.). (1978). *Mysticism and philosophical analysis*. New York: Oxford University Press.

Katz, S.T. (1983). The 'conservative' character of mystical experience. In Katz, S.T. (Ed.), *Mysticism and religious traditions* (pp. 3–60). New York: Oxford University Press.

Kelsey, M.T. (1974). *God, dreams, and revelation*. Minneapolis, MN: Augsburg.

Kelzer, K. (1987). *The sun and the shadow: My experiment with lucid dreaming*. Virginia Beach, VA: A.R.E.

King, W.L. (1980). *Theravāda meditation: The Buddhist transformation of yoga*. University Park, PA: Pennsylvania State University Press.

Krishna, G. (1970). *Kundalini: The evolutionary energy in man*. Boston, MA: Shambhala.

LaBerge, S. (1985). *Lucid dreaming*. Los Angeles, CA: Jeremy P. Tarcher.

LaBerge, S. & Rheingold, H. (1990). *Exploring the world of lucid dreaming*. New York: Ballantine Books.

Māṇḍūkya Upaniṣad.

Matus, T. (1984). *Yoga and the Jesus prayer tradition: An experiment in faith*. Ramsey, NJ: Paulist Press.

McGinn, B. (2006). *The essential writings of Christian mysticism*. New York: Modern Library.

McGinn, C. (2004). *Mindsight: Image, dream, meaning*. Cambridge, MA: Harvard University Press.

Moffitt, A., Kramer, M. & Hoffmann, R. (1993). Introduction. In A. Moffitt, M. Kramer & R. Hoffmann (Eds.). *The functions of dreaming* (pp. 1–9). Albany, NY: State University of New York Press.

Moss, K. (1985a). Experimentation with the vortex phenomenon in lucid dreams. *Lucidity Letter, 4* (1), pp. 15–16.

Moss, K. (1985b). Photographic and cinematographic applications in lucid dream control. *Lucidity Letter, 4* (2), pp. 98–103.

Müller, F.M. (1969). *The Upanishads*. (Part II). Delhi, India: Motilal Banarsidass.

Muṇḍaka Upaniṣad.

Nagel, T. (1980). What is it like to be a bat? In N. Block (Ed.), *Readings in philosophy of psychology* (Vol. 1, pp. 159–168). Cambridge, MA: Harvard University Press.

Nassau, K. (1980, October). The causes of color. *Scientific American, 243* (4), pp. 124–154.

Nathans, J. (1989, February). The genes for color vision. *Scientific American, 260* (2), pp. 42–49.

Nikhilananda, S. (1963). *The Upanishads*. New York: Harper & Row.

O'Brien, E. (1964). *Varieties of mystic experience: An anthology and interpretation.* New York: Mentor-Omega.

Otto, R. (1958). *The idea of the holy: An enquiry into the non-rational and its relation to the rational* (J.W. Harvey, Trans.). New York: Oxford University Press. (Original work published 1917.)

Palmer, P.J. (2000). *Let your life speak: Listening for the voice of vocation.* San Francisco, CA: Wiley.

Pike, N. (1992). *Mystic union: An essay in the phenomenology of mysticism.* Ithaca, NY: Cornell University Press.

Praśna Upaniṣad.

Pulver, M. (1960). The experience of light in the Gospel of St. John, in the "Corpus Hermeticum," in Gnosticism, and in the Eastern Church. In J. Campbell (Ed.), *Spiritual disciplines: Papers from the Eranos yearbooks* (pp. 239–266). Princeton, NJ: Princeton University Press.

Radhakrishnan, S. (Ed. & Trans.). (1953). *The principal Upanishads.* London: George Allen & Unwin.

Sacks, O. (1992). *Migraine* (Revised and expanded). Berkeley, CA: University of California Press.

Sacks, O. (2012). *Hallucinations.* New York: Alfred A. Knopf.

Saksena, S.K. (1971). *Nature of consciousness in Hindu philosophy.* Delhi, India: Motilal Banarsidass.

Sanford, J.A. (1989). *Dreams: God's forgotten language.* New York: HarperCollins.

Searle, J.R. (1992). *The rediscovery of the mind.* Cambridge, MA: MIT Press.

Sharma, A. (2000). Sacred scriptures and the mysticism of Advaita Vedānta. In S.T. Katz (Ed.), *Mysticism and sacred scripture* (pp. 169–183). New York: Oxford University Press.

Shepard, R.N. (1978). Externalization of mental images and the act of creation. In B.S. Randhawa & W.E. Coffman (Eds.), *Visual learning, thinking, and communication* (pp. 133–189). New York: Academic Press.

Siegel, R.K. (1977, October). Hallucinations. *Scientific American, 237* (4), pp. 132–137, 139.

Siegel, R.K. & Jarvik, M.E. (1975). Drug-induced hallucinations in animals and man. In R.K. Siegel & L.J. West (Eds.), *Hallucinations: Behavior, experience, and theory* (pp. 81–161). New York: Wiley.

Sivananda, S. (1975). *Concentration and meditation*. Shivanandanagar, India: Divine Life Society.

Smart, N. (1978). Understanding religious experience. In S. Katz (Ed.), *Mysticism and philosophical analysis* (pp. 10–21). New York: Oxford University Press.

Smart. N. (1983). The purification of consciousness and the negative path. In S. Katz (Ed.), *Mysticism and religious traditions* (pp. 117–129). New York: Oxford University Press.

Smart, N. (1996). *Dimensions of the sacred: An anatomy of the world's beliefs*. Berkeley, CA: University of California Press.

Snellgrove, D. (1987). *Indo-Tibetan Buddhism: Indian Buddhists and their Tibetan successors* (Vols. 1–2). Boston, MA: Shambhala.

Sparrow, G.S. (1976). *Lucid dreaming: Dawning of the clear light*. Virginia Beach, VA: A.R.E.

Sparrow, G.S. (1991). *Witness to his return: Personal encounters with Christ*. Virginia Beach, VA: A.R.E.

Staal, F. (1975). *Exploring mysticism: A methodological essay*. Berkeley, CA: University of California Press.

Strawson, G. (1994). The experiential and the non-experiential. In R. Warner & T. Szubka (Eds.), *The mind–body problem: A guide to the current debate* (pp. 69–86). Oxford: Blackwell.

Śvetāśvatara Upaniṣad.

Symeon the New Theologian (1980). *Symeon the new theologian: The discourses* (C.J. deCatanzaro, Trans.). Mahwah, NJ: Paulist Press.

Tart, C.T. (1969). Psychedelic experiences associated with a novel hypnotic procedure, mutual hypnosis. In C.T. Tart (Ed.), *Altered states of consciousness: A book of readings* (pp. 291–308). New York: Wiley.

Tart, C.T. (1972). Introduction to section 3. Dream consciousness. In C.T. Tart (Ed.), *Altered states of consciousness* (pp. 115–118). Garden City, NY: Doubleday.

Tart, C.T. (1975). Science, states of consciousness, and spiritual experiences: The need for state-specific sciences. In C.T. Tart (Ed.), *Transpersonal psychologies* (pp. 9–58). New York: Harper & Row.

Tart, C.T. (1984). Terminology in lucid dream research. *Lucidity Letter, 3* (1), pp. 4–6.

Teresa of Avila (1979). *Teresa of Avila: The interior castle* (K. Kavanaugh and O. Rodriguez, Trans.). New York: Paulist Press.

Tholey, P. (1988). A model for lucidity training as a means of self-healing and psychological growth. In J.I. Gackenbach & S. LaBerge (Eds.), *Conscious mind, sleeping brain: Perspectives on lucid dreaming* (pp. 263–287). New York: Plenum.

Tsongkhapa (1996). *Tsongkhapa's six yogas of Naropa* (G.H. Mullin, Ed. and Trans.). Ithaca, NY: Snow Lion.

Tsongkhapa (1997). A practice manual on the Six Yogas of Naropa: Taking the practice in hand. In G.H. Mullin (Ed. & Trans.), *Readings on the six yogas of Naropa* (pp. 99–135). Ithaca, NY: Snow Lion.

Tucci, G. (1961). *The theory and practice of the mandala: With special reference to the modern psychology of the subconscious* (A.H. Brodrick, Trans.). New York: Samuel Weiser.

Tucci, G. (1980). *The religions of Tibet* (G. Samuel, Trans.). Bombay, India: Allied. (Original work published 1970.)

Tye, M. (1996). *Ten problems of consciousness: A representational theory of the phenomenal mind.* Cambridge, MA: MIT Press.

Wayman, A. (1977). *Yoga of the Guhyasamājatantra: The arcane lore of forty verses.* Delhi, India: Motilal Banarsidass.

Woolman, J. (1971). *The journal and major essays of John Woolman* (P.P. Moulton, Ed.). New York: Oxford University Press.

Worsley, A. (1988). Personal experiences in lucid dreaming. In J.I. Gackenbach & S. LaBerge (Eds.), *Conscious mind, sleeping brain: Perspectives on lucid dreaming* (pp. 321–341). New York: Plenum.

Young, S. (1999). *Dreaming in the lotus: Buddhist dream narrative, imagery, and practice.* Boston, MA: Wisdom.

Zaehner, R.C. (Ed. & Trans.). (1966). *Hindu scriptures.* New York: Dutton.

www.ingramcontent.com/pod-product-compliance
Lightning Source LLC
Chambersburg PA
CBHW061737270326
41928CB00011B/2265

* 9 7 8 1 7 8 8 3 6 0 0 9 8 *